Pra
Spiritual Practice for Crazy Times

"Phil Goldberg is an expert, wise, calm, and profoundly compassionate guide to how to live as deeply and richly as possible in our global dark night. This book will bring true help to committed seekers on all paths."

— **Andrew Harvey**, author of *The Hope* and *Turn Me to Gold: 108 Poems of Kabir*

"From a masterful spiritual teacher comes advice for our troubled era. Phil Goldberg's Spiritual Practice for Crazy Times *is a rich resource for anyone who feels buffeted and unbalanced these days. Goldberg's wisdom is drawn from humankind's deepest spiritual traditions. You'll be wiser, more resilient, and more able to give strength to others if you rely and trust Goldberg's advice. Remember that no one survives alone. We are all in these predicaments together, and we can draw on one another's strengths. That's what this book is all about."*

— **Larry Dossey, M.D.**, author of *One Mind: How Our Individual Mind Is Part of a Greater Consciousness and Why It Matters*

"Now that we have all been thrown into the deep end, with no lifeguard on duty, here is a brilliant and useful book that will not only keep you afloat but will also guide you into the safety of the ocean of love and mercy—your own divine soul."

— **Arielle Ford**, author of *Turn Your Mate into Your Soulmate*

"This perilous moment in history calls for a practical spiritual response from each of us. In this concise and lucid book, Phil Goldberg points the way to the fortress of peace within ourselves."

— **Deepak Chopra**, author of *MetaHuman*

"Philip Goldberg's latest book is a remedy for our times. Packed with inspirational guidance and practices to uplift and strengthen us, it shows how to be peaceful inside even when the outer world is in turmoil—and respond to challenges with creativity and calm."

— **Marci Shimoff**, #1 *New York Times* best-selling author of *Happy for No Reason* and *Chicken Soup for the Woman's Soul*

"Crazy times call for crazy methods to put things right. . . . Phil Goldberg knows what he's talking about, and what goes on behind the scenes too. If anyone can bring to bear on the Path today the combined wisdom of the perennial philosophies and practical mysticism, he has the chops, as he demonstrates here. This may be his American Upanishad, a timely primer for finding timeless truths and harmony amidst the smoke and mirrors of illusion's divine dance. I enjoyed reading it and found it useful too, as will you."

— **Lama Surya Das**, author of the best-selling *Awakening the Buddha Within: Tibetan Wisdom for the Western World* and *Make Me One with Everything* and founder of the Dzogchen Center and Dzogchen Meditation retreats

"As external structures begin to collapse around us, our need to build a robust inner foundation grows more urgent. In this lucid, conversational, utterly engaging guide to contemplative methods, Phil Goldberg pays homage to the perennial wisdom traditions while skillfully translating them for this era of global crisis, so that we may become personally grounded in the storms that buffet us, as well as a source of equanimity and even joy for the greater human community."

— **Mirabai Starr**, author of *God of Love* and *Wild Mercy*

"Yes, the times are crazy, but you don't have to be. Phil Goldberg's wonderful, practical, and timeless guidance can help see to that. If you're looking for a book that will keep you sane, Spiritual Practice for Crazy Times *is it.*"

— **Rabbi Rami Shapiro**, author of *Holy Rascals: Advice for Spiritual Revolutionaries*

"This is an insightful and important book that comes at the perfect moment. Philip Goldberg offers a beautiful and practical map for finding your way through difficult and challenging times with clarity, consciousness, and steadiness. His open, authentic, and eloquent writing will be a wonderful and uplifting companion on your journey."

— **Barbara De Angelis, Ph.D.**, #1 *New York Times* best-selling author of *Soul Shifts* and *The Choice for Love*

Spiritual Practice for Crazy Times

ALSO BY PHILIP GOLDBERG

*The Life of Yogananda: The Story of the Yogi
Who Became the First Modern Guru**

*American Veda: From Emerson and the Beatles
to Yoga and Meditation, How Indian
Spirituality Changed the West*

*Roadsigns: On the Spiritual Path—
Living at the Heart of Paradox*

*The Intuitive Edge: Understanding Intuition and
Applying It in Everyday Life*

*Get Out of Your Own Way: Overcoming Self-Defeating
Behavior (with Mark Goulston, M.D.)*

*Available from Hay House

Please visit:
Hay House USA: www.hayhouse.com®
Hay House Australia: www.hayhouse.com.au
Hay House UK: www.hayhouse.co.uk
Hay House India: www.hayhouse.co.in

Spiritual Practice for Crazy Times

Powerful Tools to Cultivate Calm, Clarity, and Courage

PHILIP GOLDBERG

HAY HOUSE, INC.
Carlsbad, California • New York City
London • Sydney • New Delhi

Published In the United States by: Hay House, Inc.: www.hay house .com® • *Published in Australia by:* Hay House Australia Pty. Ltd.: www .hayhouse.com.au • *Published in the United Kingdom by:* Hay House UK, Ltd.: www.hayhouse.co.uk • *Published in India by:* Hay House Publishers India: www.hayhouse.co.in

Cover design: Claudine Mansour • *Interior design:* Nick C. Welch

Library of Congress Cataloging-in-Publication Data

Names: Goldberg, Philip, 1944- author.
Title: Spiritual practice for crazy times : powerful tools to cultivate calm, clarity, and courage / Philip Goldberg.
Identifiers: LCCN 2020011109 | ISBN 9781401959753 (hardback) ISBN 9781401959760 (ebook) / Subjects: LCSH: Spiritual life.
Classification: LCC BL624 .G63424 2020 | DDC 204--dc23
LC record available at https://lccn.loc.gov/2020011109

Tradepaper ISBN: 978-1-4019-6163-3
E-book ISBN: 978-1-4019-5976-0
Audiobook ISBN: 978-1-4019-5977-7

10 9 8 7 6 5 4 3 2 1
1st edition, August 2020

Printed in the United States of America

To all the steadfast, compassionate souls
who work to make the world a saner,
safer, and more sanctified place.

Contents

Preface

The Timing and
Timelessness
of This Book

In early 2019, not long after the mass slaughter in a Pittsburgh synagogue, when migrants were being separated from their children at the U.S.-Mexico border and the world breathlessly awaited the Mueller Report, I received an e-mail with a cartoon attached. It was by David Sipress, whose insightful art was frequently featured in the *New Yorker* magazine. Two people are walking on a city street. One says to the other, "My desire to be well-informed is currently at odds with my desire to remain sane."

Bingo! I immediately forwarded the cartoon to friends and posted it on social media. Turns out I was not the only one; the joke had gone viral because it captured a prevalent mood. Terms like *overwhelmed*, *confused*, *helpless*, *afraid*, *enraged*, and *despondent* were common, even among veterans of the spiritual path whose outlook was usually upbeat. That prompted me to write an article titled "The Importance of Spiritual Practice in Crazy Times." I argued that spiritual practices were an absolute necessity in times like these for two reasons: they provide a much-needed sanctuary when we need it most, and they're also a sturdy platform for corrective action. The response to the article and affirmation of its basic premise led me to start this book.

Then came an interesting twist. When I searched online for the Sipress cartoon so I could properly reference it, I found an essay by the artist himself. He said that, of all his many cartoons, that one was "the most published, republished, tweeted, retweeted, liked, shared, or stolen and reprinted without my permission." The essay was dated February 3, 2017—two whole years before the cartoon arrived in my inbox! Ah, but that was only two weeks after Donald Trump's inauguration, when much of the world was in shock and therapists were reporting that their clients were self-medicating and ranting about politics instead of their usual issues.

But here's the *real* shocker. Sipress had originally published that cartoon in the 1990s, during the Clinton Administration. Ever since, he said, "every time the news gets particularly dire, the cartoon pops up all over the place."

Which highlights an important point I want to emphasize at the outset. It has been said that we live in uniquely crazy times—in many ways we surely do, a 2018 Gallup poll, for instance, found that the level of stress, anger, and worry in America was the highest it had been in a decade. But sociopolitical turmoil has no deadlines or expiration dates. We've endured it repeatedly, and we'll deal with it again, no matter who is president or which new crises humans create for themselves. Furthermore, for each of us, *any* time can be a crazy time. Many of the conditions that make us feel emotionally assaulted, angry, helpless, and exhausted are endemic to modern life. In our plugged-in, fast-paced world, high stress levels are more predictable than the weather, and a crisis can rise up and assault anyone at any time.

For that reason, this book is not designed for this wild and woolly era alone. The advice, insights, and practices it contains are perennial; they will be as relevant in 2040 and 2080 as they are in 2020. They cut across cultural and spiritual categories, and their value does not depend on our beliefs or affiliations. Whenever mayhem arises, the practical methods in this book can be counted on for refuge, firm footing, and transformation.

And, I hasten to add, the information and guidelines you're about to explore will be just as useful when times are good. They are the spiritual equivalent of good nutrition and exercise—ongoing maintenance and wellness enhancement for the soul. Regardless of your spiritual orientation and current life circumstances, you will find the book a valuable companion on your spiritual path. May it accelerate your progress on the sacred journey we all traverse together.

ADDENDUM

It is March 2020, and I am examining the galley proofs of this book while much of the world is engaged in social distancing to combat the coronavirus pandemic. If ever there was proof that crazy times can get crazier at a moment's notice, and that spiritual practices are a necessity not a luxury, this is it. My editor and I decided not to change a word of the text in response to the crisis. The information applies now, and it will still apply no matter what transpires in the five months before publication.

CHAPTER 1

The Times,
They Are a-Crazy

Step Up to Spiritual Sanity

*While ponderous planets of unwaning woe revolve
round me, deep down and deep inland there I
still bathe me in eternal mildness of joy.*

— HERMAN MELVILLE, *Moby-Dick*

In the late 1960s, I was a dazed and confused
young man trying to figure out how to live in a
world gone mad. Vietnam, assassinations, riots, and
other horrors made coming of age feel like a life-or-
death issue.

One day, I found myself alone in a gallery of
Buddhist statues in the Boston Museum of Fine Arts.
It was called the Temple Room, and it felt like one.
As I moved slowly from one work of art to another,

I was profoundly and irrevocably touched by the serene faces of the Buddhas. *Whatever those guys had,* I thought, *I want it.*

I soon learned more about what those guys had as, in the course of my seeking, I read the Bhagavad Gita. One passage in India's great sacred text seized my attention like a hand clasping my shoulder from behind. It said that advanced yogis have "equanimity in gain and loss, victory and defeat, pleasure and pain."[1] That was exactly what I wanted: equanimity, defined as "mental calmness, composure, and evenness of temper, especially in a difficult situation."

Those twin impressions—the faces and the words—were crucial factors in launching me on my spiritual path. The promise sounded awfully good to me.

Doesn't it sound good to you?

THE PROMISE AND THE PREMISE

The key ingredient in a recipe for equanimity is spiritual practice. And in crazy times like ours, we need prayer, meditation, mindfulness, and other practices more than ever. They are not luxury items like a vacation; they're more akin to necessities. Think of it: When times are tough, do our bodies,

---

[1] From Chapter 2, verse 38.

minds, and souls need healing, rejuvenation, and nourishment? Do we need periods of silence to neutralize the incessant noise? Tournaments of light to counter the dark energies afoot? A stabilizing anchor when the winds of rancor and rage are swirling?

Of course we do.

Yet, when I first started talking and writing about this subject, I was surprised to hear objections from people who normally placed a high value on spiritual practice. Some said they were too riled up by what's going on in the world to center themselves with their usual rituals. Others said they were too busy trying to make a dent in our many social problems. "I don't want to waste time on my inner life when there's so much at stake out there," one activist told me. She was afraid she'd lose her edge if her anger and angst were replaced by calm, and she didn't want to take her mind off the task at hand.

To the first set of reasons, I said: Waiting until you're calm and clear before you sit to meditate is like showering only when you're clean. Thinking you're too agitated to pray or do Yoga exercises is like believing you're too sick to see a doctor or too tired to take a nap. We need self-protection in turbulent times even more than we usually do.

To the second set of reasons, and to the dedicated souls who are working hard to change the world,

I say this: Spiritual methodologies are a boon to engaged citizenship and a blessing to our collective well-being. They're not tranquilizers that turn practitioners into complacent blobs. They don't make you a grinning blissball who runs around spouting platitudes about God's will. In fact, deep spirituality can be a foundation for smart, robust action. Think of Mahatma Gandhi, Martin Luther King Jr., and the revered saints in every culture who were also powerful rulers, warriors, and social reformers.

I made that argument to the activist who thought spirituality was incompatible with social engagement. I even invoked a spiritual teacher she respected, Paramahansa Yogananda. Having thoroughly researched Yogananda's life for my biography of him,[2] I knew that he exemplified my premise. He was an orange-robed monk, but he worked harder than most C.E.O.s and was acutely aware of world affairs, speaking out against injustice, bigotry, colonialism, and other ills of his era. He revered reformers like Gandhi who took righteous action "while inwardly united with the joy of Spirit," as he put it.

My friend was certainly right that indignation and outrage can be useful catalysts for social action. But only to a point. An overly agitated mind is prone to mistakes. If we lack a calm center, rage can turn us into blind ship captains trying to navigate in a

---

[2]   *The Life of Yogananda: The Story of the Yogi Who Became the First Modern Guru* (Hay House, 2018).

violent storm. Ask a business leader or a police officer how he or she wants to be when swift decisions and immediate actions are demanded: frantic and unsteady or cool and collected? Soldiers retreat to safe places to regroup and restore their strength. Athletes do the same; we call it halftime.

Spiritual practice serves a similar function in an active life. It not only provides relief, it produces desirable qualities such as composure, compassion, alertness, and resilience. Over time, it can create an inner fortress—a safe haven, a vantage point for heightened awareness, and a staging ground for skillful engagement.

In short, the spiritual is practical. Investing the time to fortify our connection to our Divine Source and unfold vital inner qualities is among the most pragmatic of all human endeavors. "My spiritual life is not . . . a fenced-off devotional patch rather difficult to cultivate, and needing to be sheltered from the cold winds of the outer world," wrote the eminent scholar of religion Evelyn Underhill a century ago. "Nor is it an alternative to my outward, practical life. On the contrary, it is the very source of that quality and purpose which makes my practical life worthwhile."

That basic premise has been validated in millions of lives over eons of time, as well as by a growing body of scientific research. Spiritual practice in crazy times is not just a rest stop, but a refueling station; not a mere escape valve, but a launching pad.

IT'S AN INSIDE JOB

Where are you searching for me, friend?
Look! Here am I right within you.
Not in temple, nor in mosque, not in Kaaba,
nor Kailas, but here right within you am I.

— KABIR

By far the most stable, dependable, secure, and impenetrable sanctuary is not a place we have to locate, like the nearest chapel; not something we have to search for, like a calm harbor to anchor in; not something we have to construct, like a storm cellar in the basement. Nor is it something to be obtained, like a medicine or a massage. It doesn't have to be achieved, acquired, or earned. It is your birthright. You already have it. It is within you, deep inside, at the core of your being. The sanctuary of perfect peace is your inherent nature. It is your true Self, abiding above, beneath, beyond, and within the personality you normally think of as "me" and "I"—the one that walks, talks, and acts through the singular form called your body. It is what T. S. Eliot called "the still point of the turning world." It is the

Self of all selves, and it is closer than your breath, nearer than your heartbeat.

The sages of every spiritual tradition have described that inner sanctum, pointed to the entrance, given us the keys, and implored us—sometimes gently, sometimes fervently—to enter and abide. Here you will find a balm for your beleaguered mind, body, and soul, they have promised. Open up to it, absorb it, and then return to outer life suffused anew with energy, power, and perspective. Now you can do what needs to be done with greater proficiency and wisdom.

That last point can't be emphasized enough. Over the course of history, people devoted to spiritual attainment have been disparaged as otherworldly. They've been called self-obsessed, apathetic escapists. They've been vilified for being so focused on personal salvation that they're indifferent to, or naïve about, the social conditions that cause human suffering. Sadly, this impression has often been reinforced by spiritual aspirants who *do* withdraw from worldly affairs and by spiritual teachers who *do* encourage disengagement.

Make no mistake, renunciation has a treasured place in the spiritual life. It is indispensable as a temporary respite and a periodic source of deepening. And as a way of life for vow-taking monastics who divorce themselves from family and commerce, it deserves the utmost respect. But linking spirituality with passivity and retreat is a misconception. In fact, even most monastics are busy doing good for others through some form of service; very few are out-and-out hermits.

So let's agree to separate "spiritual" from erroneous associations like apathy, superstition, and meekness. Let's think of the term as shorthand for qualities like deep, enduring, essential, timeless, wholeness, and transformation. Forget the stereotype of lethargic space cadets. Think instead of spiritual discipline as a necessary preparation for vigorous action, like stretching your hamstrings before a run or scrubbing your hands before surgery.

This is the central message of the Hero's Journey,[3] a persistent theme in storytelling throughout human history: the hero retreats from society's tumult, undergoes a spiritual transformation, and returns to the world better equipped to serve the greater good. The hero of the Bhagavad Gita, that most sensible of sacred texts, is an esteemed warrior, not a wandering mendicant. He, Arjuna, is immobilized by indecision at the beginning of the tale, and Krishna—the embodiment of divine wisdom in the form of Arjuna's friend and charioteer—does

---

[3]   See *The Hero with a Thousand Faces* by Joseph Campbell, first published in 1949 by Pantheon Press and reissued in 2008 by New World Library.

not advise him to run away to an ashram or cave. No, he tells Arjuna to rise up and do his duty, which in this case means to vanquish the forces of evil, even though some of the bad guys are his own relatives. We are all Arjunas, whether our battlefield is a boardroom, a kitchen, a classroom, an election, or a blank page like the one I'm facing now.

STRATEGY FOR SPIRITUAL SANITY

The aim of this book is to provide the tools you need to ward off the ravages of modern life—and the spiritual weapons to fight back against destructive forces. The top priority, addressed in the next two chapters, is to help you establish a personal spiritual routine—what yogis call a *sadhana*—that connects you to the ultimate source of strength and stability within. Subsequent chapters will supplement those core practices with a repertoire of methods you can call upon according to your needs and the amount of time you have available. Having established that arsenal of practices, we'll address ways to rearrange your surroundings, rethink your lifestyle, and upgrade your relationships for maximum protection and spiritual growth. We'll also consider ways to adjust your mind-set and your habitual reactions to outside events. And we'll give special attention to ways of protecting yourself when you're slammed by a personal crisis or a social upheaval. The final chapter focuses on the benefits, and the necessity, of using your spiritual gifts to make the world a little less crazy.

Some of the techniques in the book employ the faculties of mind and intellect; some are physical, involving breath or movement; some engage the emotional dimension of our lives; and some are behavioral or relational, meaning they focus on how we engage with other people and the world at large. The categories are just reference points. All aspects of our lives are interrelated; like the legs of a table, if one is moved, the others move as well. And all the practices, not just the obvious ones like meditation and prayer, are *spiritual* because their intent is to unite our conscious awareness with the infinite Reality that is our essential nature.

There is nothing pie-in-the-sky about this; abundant evidence indicates that spiritual practice adds concrete value to one's life. The proof is laid out in the sacred texts of every tradition, and it's supported by the testimony of practitioners throughout recorded history. In recent times, convincing evidence has been gathered by neuroscientists and other researchers who have measured the effects of mindfulness, meditation, prayer, and other methodologies. Their findings clearly show that techniques traditionally considered "spiritual" enliven the mind, calm the body, open the heart to positive emotions (compassion, empathy, love, etc.), heal the ravages of accumulated stress, and, in general, nudge behavior patterns in the directions we regard as desirable. That's why physicians and psychotherapists commonly recommend secular versions of these methods, a trend that would have been unthinkable not very long ago.

YOUR WAY ON THE HIGHWAY

Throughout the book you will find instructions, exercises, guidelines, and recommendations—but no one-size-fits-all formula. As India's sages told us centuries ago, all spiritual pathways eventually converge on the peak of Oneness. And on the way up, the smoothest and swiftest progress comes when each of us is empowered to make informed decisions based on our personal needs, predilections, and circumstances. The book will help you make discerning decisions as you explore the diverse, sometimes bewildering spiritual marketplace. I urge you to make your choices in the spirit of experimentation, as if doing lab work to test a hypothesis or a new technology.

Needless to say, I could not include every potentially useful method without turning the book into an encyclopedia. Hence, you are encouraged to poke around and add to your spiritual pantry any ingredients you find useful.

The book draws from the mystical, or esoteric, components of the sacred traditions. By that I mean the internal dimension of spiritual experience, as opposed to the outward-facing aspects of religion such as doctrines, creeds, and observances. Our principal concern is with experience and transformation, not dogma or belief systems. If you need a name for this approach, call it *pragmatic mysticism.* Not "mysticism" in the otherworldly sense, but defined this way (by Merriam-Webster): "the experience of mystical union or direct communion with ultimate reality reported by mystics." And "pragmatic" because it connotes realistic, sensible, hardheaded, down-to-earth, and practical. The book aims to be useful to people with responsibilities, desires, and worldly concerns by helping them attune to the limitless energy and intelligence that created the universe and keeps it running.

As many scholars have documented, the spiritual experiences of mystics across eras and cultures are strikingly similar to one another, even though their practices, imagery, and languages vary. Hence, the 15th-century Christian mystic Nicholas of Cusa could say, "To know the sweetness of the Infinite within us, that is the cause, the reason, the pur pose, the *only* purpose of our being." And in Japan, two centuries earlier, the Zen master Dōgen could put it this way: "Everyone holds a precious jewel, all embrace a special gem; if you do not turn your attention around and look within, you will wander from home with a hidden treasure."

While the book recognizes the common essence of all traditions, it draws especially on the insights of India's ancient sages and the methods that evolved from their exploration. Rather than make academic distinctions among the various subtraditions the West has lumped together under the rubric "Hinduism,"[4] I use the term Yoga (and the adjective yogic), because Yoga can be viewed as a spiritual science applicable to anyone's life, as its adoption by people of all religions and no religion attests. The very word *Yoga*, with its origin in the Sanskrit root that gave us *yoke*, connotes unity—not the union of the head and the knee, mind you, but of the finite personal self and the cosmic Self that is our Source. Yogic practices are designed to cultivate awareness of that Oneness while also producing immediate benefits for the mind and body.

---

[4] Many Indians prefer the term *Sanatana Dharma* (usually translated as Eternal Way) to "Hinduism," which they regard as a colonial imposition.

The book's approach is captured in a key phrase in the Bhagavad Gita: "Established in Yoga, perform action."[5] It's a Spiritual Two-Step: (1) turn within for the Divine Unity we all seek, like rivers meandering to the sea; (2) come out stronger, more stable, more conscious, more compassionate, and more attuned— and therefore more capable. It is not a huge leap to conclude that this was basically the same practical advice Jesus had in mind when he implored his followers, "Seek ye first the Kingdom of God, and his righteousness; and all these things shall be added unto you" (Matthew 6:33).

KEEP IT REAL

Think of spiritual practices as technologies. As with all worthwhile technologies, the proof is in the pudding, and in this case the pudding is tangible benefit to your life. It doesn't matter what you believe or don't believe. It doesn't matter whether you have confidence in the methods themselves. Just as smartphones, automobiles, televisions, and refrigerators work for anyone who uses them properly, the spiritual techniques in this book work equally well if you're a devout believer in a mainstream religion,

---

[5]   Chapter 2, verse 48.

a member of an offbeat sect, an atheist, an agnostic, or "spiritual but not religious."

I suggest you give the practices a fair chance to work, and evaluate them objectively. As the subtitle of this book suggests, they should help you cultivate and maintain calmness, clarity, and courage in the midst of crazy times. Beyond that, keep your eye out for enhanced compassion and empathy, a clearer mind, greater resilience and equanimity, deeper connections with others, a stronger sense of wholeness, a whole lot less fear, and a heightened capacity for love. All of which will give you a sturdy anchor in the crazy whirlwind we have to navigate every day.

While you're observing and evaluating, try to be patient. Remember those Buddhist statues that helped launch my spiritual life? If those deeply contented expressions once graced the faces of actual people, they did not get that way overnight. Spiritual progress tends to be slow and steady; the path often winds through detours, U-turns, and potholes. The gains you make are likely to show up incrementally, not all at once in a lightning bolt of awakening from which you will never come down. There might also appear to be setbacks. But the journey as a whole is ever evolving. If you're diligent and persistent, you can count on steady upward progress.

I learned the importance of patience and realistic expectations in two ways: from hundreds of interviews with spiritual seekers for my books and podcast (*Spirit Matters*); and from my own painful, often comedic, experiences.

For example, that Bhagavad Gita passage I mentioned at the outset, the one that promised equanimity in loss and gain, victory and defeat, pleasure and pain. I wanted that equanimity so badly that, subconsciously, I interpreted the words to mean that all I had to do was keep meditating and breathing and doing Yoga exercises and a time would come—pretty damn soon—when I would no longer experience loss, defeat, or pain.

Imagine my surprise. I learned the hard way that spiritual practice is not like a pesticide that destroys or drives away the pesky aspects of life. It's more like an immune booster or a sturdy garment that keeps us dry and warm in a blizzard. The promise is not the absence of outrageous slings and arrows but the presence of peace, perhaps even joy, in the midst of the inevitable madness. It's a declaration of independence from the ravages of life, and it's strictly an inside job.

In the naïve period of my path, I reacted to bumps in the road with incredulity, like "What is that doing here? It's supposed to be smooth and carefree!" In time I noticed the true signs of growth when a adult hit the profession for, I was less overwhelmed than I would have been in the past. I might still worry or get mad, but with less intensity. I also reclaimed my center far more quickly, and was thereby able to take remedial action instead of getting so flummoxed, so agitated, that I'd make things worse.

Before I acquired a spiritual repertoire, traumas and minor disturbances would—to use a yogic metaphor—imprint my nervous system like a line etched in stone with a sharp knife. They cut deep, and their impact persisted. Later, as I progressed, they were more like lines carved into soil, and eventually (sometimes at least) like lines in sand. I may never reach the standard of sloughing off upsets like lines drawn in water, much less air, but the steady progress is undeniable, and its value is beyond measure.[6] That's what this book can confidently promise: not the fantasy of no more craziness, but ever-increasing stability, peace, and steadiness of mind in the midst of whatever comes along.

---

[6] Actually, it *has* been measured: faster recovery from stress is one of the consistent findings in research on meditative practices.

CHAPTER 2

Turn Off, Tune Out, Drop In

The Power of Deep Meditation

*At the center of our being is a
point of nothingness which is
untouched by sin and by illusion,
a point of pure truth, a point or spark
which belongs entirely to God.*

— THOMAS MERTON

On the morning I started work on this chapter, I threw on a random T-shirt from a drawer, filled a thermos with tea, and walked to my office. On the glass door, I saw my reflection. Through some act of grace, karma, or chance, this was imprinted on my shirt:

MEDITATION IT'S NOT WHAT YOU THINK

The inscription contains three profound messages:

1. Meditation may not be what you think it is.

2. The effectiveness of meditation has nothing to do with the content of thoughts that arise in the mind.

3. At its deepest, meditation transcends thinking entirely, opening the curtain to the infinite Oneness beyond the mind. It's a direct route to the core of Being.

That last point is why so many teachings advocate some form of meditative practice as the centerpiece of an effective spiritual routine. Once you learn a method that suits you, you can introduce into daily life an upgrade on Timothy Leary's LSD-soaked clarion call from the 1960s. Instead of "Turn on, tune in, drop out," you can "Turn off, tune out, drop in"—as in, turn off your devices and your media hookups, tune out the incessant barrage of news and sensory stimulation, and drop in to the sanctuary, or Kingdom, within you. We could also add "come back" to that dictum—as in come back to the domain of action rejuvenated and spiritually energized.

In this chapter, you'll learn two types of meditation practice, one utilizing the breath and the other internal sound in the form of a mantra. First, some important preliminary information.

WHAT IT IS AND WHAT IT'S NOT

More than half a century ago, the Beatles took up Transcendental Meditation, thousands of their fans followed suit, and curious scientists did studies to see what all the fuss was about. Meditation entered the mainstream on the wings of their data. Now there are more meditation techniques on the market than breakfast cereals, and if that's not confusing enough, the media make things worse with simplistic and misinformed coverage. So let's clear up some misconceptions before we move on to practical instructions.[7]

For starters, the various types of meditation should not be lumped together as if they were all the same. Is it logical to assume that techniques that are practiced differently would produce the same outcomes? Not really. Similar, perhaps, but not identical, like apple pies made from different recipes.

How do meditation techniques differ? For one thing, the various methods utilize different objects

---

[7]   If you already have a meditation practice you're happy with, terrific. I suggest you read the rest of the chapter anyway, as it might deepen your understanding.

of attention—some the breath, others a mantra, a prayerful phrase, a visualization, or a location within the body—and some use no focal point at all. Methods also vary in the degree of effort they entail. Some demand rigorous mind control; others are less strenuous but require a certain amount of effort to focus or concentrate; and still others emphasize ease, effortlessness, and release of mental control. Each variation has value, but their differences should not be underestimated.

Public discussion of meditation is also muddied by loose language. For example, many "contemplative" Christian and Jewish practices do not involve contemplation in the usual sense, i.e., reflecting on the meaning of something. Instead, they're more like Eastern meditation techniques that don't involve pondering or discursive thinking at all. Also, some practices labeled "prayer"—chief among them Centering Prayer—do not entail what we usually think of as praying; they're meditative practices that take the mind beyond words to communion with the Divine. Perhaps most confusing of all, the word *mindfulness* is often used mindlessly, sometimes as a synonym for meditation, sometimes as an umbrella term for all practices that involve the use of attention, and sometimes specifically for methods that derive from Buddhism (we'll return to this shortly). As a result, something called mindfulness might be a meditation practice, but it could also be something quite different.

Confused? Don't worry about it. Just keep these nuances in mind so you can be discerning as you explore the various options.

Now let's address an issue that often comes up. "I can't meditate," people tell me. "My mind is a cacophony of thoughts. I'm just not the meditating type."

It's an understandable concern, but an erroneous one. You see, *everyone's* mind bubbles with thoughts. Buddhists call it monkey mind, and we all have it. Unfortunately, when people hear that meditation quiets the mind, they find that prospect appealing, so they sit down and try to force their minds to shut up . . . and they can't. So they try harder. No dice. The harder they try, the more frustrated they get. So they figure they're just not cut out for this sort of thing.

The wiser conclusion would be: "I need some expert instruction." I find it amazing that people who wouldn't dream of trying to fly a plane, or program a computer, or play the saxophone without first learning how to do it would think they can go do-it-yourself into meditation.

The fact is, *anyone can learn to meditate.* I repeat: anyone. The mind thinks. That's its job. But, like the surface of a lake that fluctuates as the wind shifts—violent waves, choppy ripples, rolling swells, placid stillness—sometimes the mind is frenetic, sometimes just a bit revved up, sometimes kind of quiet, and sometimes pretty darn tranquil. Well, the mind can become *far more quiet* than you might imagine. It can even settle into pure silence if you know how to let it.

Meditation dials down the mind from frenzied to serene. And, over time, that meditative quiet carries into active life. That's why the equanimity we discussed earlier can be felt even when life is hectic and the mind is stirred, just as the depths of a lake remain still when the surface is churning. But you have to learn how.

LEARNING TO MEDITATE

The instructions that follow are not meant to substitute for expert personal guidance. In my experience, meditation is best learned from a well-trained teacher. Written instructions can be misinterpreted. The printed page can't answer immediate questions. Audio or video instruction is a step up, but that too has shortcomings. There is simply no substitute for a qualified instructor who can respond to experiences and concerns as they arise. So I encourage you to find a reputable teacher of a meditation technique that appeals to you.

That said, the instructions that follow will give you a significant experience of two common meditation forms, one utilizing breath awareness, the other using a mantra. If you follow the guidelines correctly, beneficial results will surely follow.

As I explained earlier, meditation practices use varying degrees of effort. For the practices I'll describe here, I have chosen gentle ease over control or exertion. There are two reasons for this.

First, in my experience, methods that call for rigorous concentration are best practiced in the context of ongoing supervision to avoid the hazards of excessive strain.

Second, the less intense the effort, the more direct the route to the inner sanctuary. Here's why. Attempting to restrain the mind, or coercing it to sit still as if training a disobedient dog, can agitate instead of calm. It's like trying to stop your car while pushing the gas pedal at the same time. Instead, we can gently point the wandering mind to the happiness it instinctively seeks. We are bliss-seeking missiles, drawn to the Infinite like a plant is drawn to the sun. Effortless practice recognizes this tendency and lets nature lead the way to the sublime contentment of our eternal Source, whose nature, the yogis have discovered, is bliss (in Sanskrit, *ananda*).

That is the basic rationale for favoring low-effort, non-force styles of meditation, especially in the absence of ongoing supervision. As they say in the Zen tradition, if you want to clear up muddy water, just leave it alone.

Now let's meditate.

Minding the Breath

Mindfulness is broadly defined as bringing one's attention to present-moment experience without judging or conceptualizing. Classic mindfulness practices derive from Buddhist teachings. Some are done with eyes open, some with eyes closed; some employ sustained concentration, some encourage unforced focus; some are done while active, others in seated meditation. Here are instructions for the most widely used mindfulness meditation. It involves focusing easily on the breath.

Begin by sitting comfortably on a stable seat. If you're in a chair, place your feet flat on the floor; if on a cushion, sit cross-legged or with legs outstretched.

Sit with your back and neck straight, but remain comfortable—not in a posture that requires effort or strain to maintain.

Rest your hands on your legs in a natural position. Traditionally, palms up is recommended, either with each hand on the corresponding thigh or with both hands in your lap and the left resting in the right.

Now you have a choice: close your eyes or keep them open, Zen-style. If you want to try the latter, lower your chin a little, soften your gaze, and focus easily on the ground three to six feet in front of you.

If you wish, try the suggestion of the Vietnamese Buddhist monk Thich Nhat Hanh: bring a half-smile to your face (as Buddha is depicted in traditional art).

Now bring your attention to the physical sensation of breathing. Focus on the air entering and leaving your nostrils (most teachers recommend nasal breathing) and/or the rise and fall of your diaphragm and chest.

Without straining, rest your focus on the natural in-breath and out-breath. Do not breathe in any particular way or in a predetermined pattern. The idea is not to control the breath but simply to observe it. "As for everything else," says Thich Nhat Hanh, "let it go."

Remain in the present moment with your attention on your breath. Your mind will inevitably wander; don't expect it not to. Just observe the thoughts and sensations that arise without judgment—and if judgments arise, don't judge them either. When you notice your attention has left your breath, easily and gently direct it to return.

Continue in this manner for a preset period of time (15–20 minutes is a good starting place). When your time expires, take at least a minute or two to transition to active life. When you feel ready, gently open your eyes or lift your gaze. Note the difference between the pre- and postmeditation state of your mind, body, and emotions.

Mantra Meditation

Now we segue to a meditation style that's more mind*emptiness* than mindfulness: effortless meditation with mantras. The ancient science of utilizing sound vibrations to produce a beneficial effect gave rise to the now-familiar use of Sanskrit mantras in meditation. The mantras employed by different teaching lineages vary, as do the ways they are used in practice. Some intone mantras internally in rhythmic fashion similar to chanting aloud; some repeat syllables for a set number of counts; some coordinate repetitions with the in-breath and out-breath; some locate the mantra sound in a part of the body, typically the center of the chest or between the eyebrows.[8] The form we're about to do involves none of that: no attempt to sustain focus or concentrate, no mind control, and will power - all trying to do anything. It's as close to effortless as a method can be.

Typically, teachers select mantras for specific students based on certain criteria, which vary from one tradition to another. Here we'll use this one: *so hum*. Its meaning is not really relevant for our purposes (it's the sound vibration that matters), but for the record it is usually translated as "I am That."[9]

I suggest studying the instructions that follow before you do the practice so you don't have to open your eyes to read once you begin (but feel free to peek if necessary).

Sit in a comfortable position, cross-legged or in a chair with your feet flat on the floor.

Keep your back and neck straight to the extent you can do so without strain.

Close your eyes and take half a minute or so to settle in. Allow any bodily tension to dissipate.

Now, with lips closed, gently and easily intone *so hum* internally.

---

[8]   These locations are associated with two of the seven chakras, or subtle energy centers: the heart or *anahata* chakra and the *ajna* chakra, a.k.a. the "third eye," which is associated with intuitive knowing.

[9]   "That" signifies the Self that is not separate from Ultimate Reality. "I am That" is the self-referential equivalent of the famous statement in the Upanishads, *tat tvam asi*, or "Thou art That."

Using only the faintest intention, with as little effort as you would use to think of your name, allow the mantra to repeat.

Continue in that way, making no attempt to maintain a particular rhythm or volume. Not even a consistent pronunciation. Just effortlessly introduce the vibration of the mantra and allow it to resonate within you in whatever form it naturally assumes. If it becomes a soft, vague hum, that's fine. If it gets loud and clear, also fine.

When you notice the mantra is starting to fade away, let it go. Don't clutch or cling. Just release and enjoy the silence.

When you feel comfortable reintroducing the mantra, do so in that same noneffortful way.

During meditation, thoughts, sensations, and feelings will come and go. Let them. Don't resist or try to suppress them, and don't wish they weren't there. Treat positive, uplifting thoughts and dark, disturbing thoughts exactly the same way—as clouds drifting past the sun or debris blowing past your window on a windy day.

Remember: attempting to manipulate, control, or force will produce agitation, not the stillness we seek. So will *trying* to produce that stillness.

A typical meditation session will fluctuate between quiet periods and hurly-burly mental activity. Your only job is to innocently introduce the mantra and allow it to reverberate within. As long as you do that effortlessly, you're meditating correctly.

Note that even a relatively turbulent meditation still produces benefits, because surges of restlessness usually indicate that the system is cleansing itself of internalized traumas and accumulated stress.

When your session is over (again, 15–20 minutes is a reasonable length to begin with), stop intentionally repeating the mantra. Shift your attention to neutral and take a few minutes before you open your eyes. If you feel like stretching or massaging a body part, or lying down, go ahead. Generally speaking, you will usually feel more relaxed, alert, and at peace than you did before meditation. When you're ready, open your eyes slowly, and gently rise to take on the day.

The Silence of the Gap

What we are looking for is what is looking.

— St. Francis of Assisi

One experience that might occur during meditation deserves mention before we move on. You may notice moments of pure silence—gaps, however brief, between thoughts, when you are conscious but not conscious *of* anything. No ideas, no sensations, no mantra. Just Awareness. This experience might be so fleeting, so ephemeral, that it doesn't even register. But if you notice it has occurred, you should understand what's going on.

Yogis call that state of pure consciousness *turiya,* which means "fourth." Why fourth? Because it is different from our usual three states of consciousness: waking, dreaming, and sleeping. It is a state of Being, of I-ness, in which you are in deep repose but neither asleep nor dreaming. You are awake but not in the ordinary waking state of thinking, feeling, and doing. It's as if you were watching a movie, caught up in the flickering images, and suddenly the projector stops. Now you're aware of the screen itself. The state is also a form of *samadhi,* in which consciousness is revealed in its pure state, free of all content. As suggested earlier, some biblical interpreters equate this with Jesus's Kingdom of God. The terminology doesn't matter; what matters is that it is a state of deep contentment, and even when the experience is momentary, it has profound practical implications.

Transcending mental activity in this manner frees up the part of you—call it your soul if you wish—that is already safe, already at peace, already untouched by the turbulence of worldly life. This is the sanctuary of Self we discussed earlier, what the ancient Taoists called "the palace of nowhere." It is also a wellspring of energy and intelligence. Each time we tap into that limitless resource, some of those desirable qualities cling, and over time they manifest more and more in our active lives. Maharishi Mahesh Yogi, with whom I studied, compared this developmental process to the traditional Indian way of creating colorful fabrics. A colorless cloth is saturated with dye. Then it's placed in the sun, and by end of the day only a little color remains. Next day it's dyed again and bleached again. Now the remaining color is a bit more vivid. The sequence is repeated—dye, bleach, dye, bleach—until the desired color is permanently fixed.

You may have already tasted that silence in meditation, and if you haven't, you probably will. You may also (or instead) have noticed it at unexpected times while you're active—stillness coexisting with ordinary thought, sensation, speech, and motion. Do you recall moments, however fleeting, when the part of you that doesn't change—that is always "I" and always aware—was witnessing your mind and body think and speak and do stuff? When you realized that you are a being of pure Spirit taking a joyride in a rented vehicle called your body?

That witness is the deathless Self that is always present, albeit unrecognized, while your finite persona is busy with its life. This is described in a famous metaphor from the Upanishads: "The ego [the individual personality] and the Self dwell as intimate friends in the same body, like two golden birds perched in the same tree. The ego eats the sweet and sour fruits of the tree, while the Self looks on detached." The passage goes on to explain the implications: "For as long as you identify with the ego, you will feel joy and sorrow. But if you know you are the Self, the Lord of Life, you will be free from suffering."[10]

If your meditation provides glimpses of that unitive state, be glad. But don't be disappointed if it doesn't. Don't look for it. Don't try to make it happen. The effort will actually keep it from happening, just as trying to force sleep to come or coerce someone into falling in love with you will typically backfire. Think of it as grace. It comes unpredictably, and we can no more control it than we can control the wind. What we *can* do is invite it in by creating the right conditions. As a Zen master once said, "Enlightenment is an accident, and meditation makes you accident prone."

---

[10]   Mundaka Upanishad, Chapter 3.

Additional Guidelines

- I recommend making a meditation practice that works for you the centerpiece of a regular spiritual routine, or sadhana. This doesn't have to be a long-term commitment; our spiritual needs can change. If you decide to try out different methods, practice them one at a time as opposed to mixing them up in any given session.

- Treat meditation as part of your daily customs—a necessity like showering or brushing your teeth.

- At the same time, make it a *special* routine, not one you perform with indifference merely out of habit. When you sit to meditate, treat the moment as sacred.

- Meditate for a set period of time. Twenty minutes twice a day has become an accepted formula. But there is nothing sacrosanct about that. Do what best fits your circumstances, and apply the Goldilocks Principle: not too short, not too long; not too seldom, not too often.

- It's okay to peek at a clock to see if the time is up. If you use a timer, make it a soft tone, not an alarming alarm.

- As for *when* to meditate, there is no better way to start the day. After your morning ablutions and before breakfast is usually recommended (meditating on a full stomach is not advised, because the practice lowers metabolism and therefore conflicts with digestive needs). As for a second period later in the day, some prescribe after work and before dinner; others say closer to bedtime.

- You can meditate anywhere you can sit, but some places are obviously more conducive than others. A dedicated room, or a space within a room, is desirable but far from necessary. The quieter the better, but absolute silence is hard to come by, and a little noise is not a deterrent.

- Prevent disturbances if you can. Shut off your devices. Close your door, and train your family, housemates, and pets to stay out.

- If you have a dedicated space, you might want to add some inspiring accoutrements, e.g., sacred artifacts, objects of art, an altar with photos of spiritual exemplars and/or loved ones. If you find items like candles and incense soothing, by all means use them. Music (especially with lyrics) is not recommended, as it will draw your attention outward.

- Before beginning, you might want to sanctify the moment. Perhaps recite a prayer—one of your own or one from a sacred tradition. Or utter an invocation that expresses your intent. Try completing one of these sentences: "I enter into meditation for the purpose of . . ." "May this practice bring . . ." "I dedicate this meditation to . . ."

- A reminder about posture: Sitting with the back and neck straight is recommended, but without straining. A firm cushion or chair is advisable; if your seat is too soft, you'll slouch. Use whatever back support helps you sit straight. Comfort above all.

IF YOU EXPLORE FURTHER

Should you decide you want to look into meditation techniques not in this book, don't leave home without your discernment. Here's some advice:

- If you prefer a practice rooted in your religion, you would do well to turn to the mystical branches: Muslims to the Sufi tradition and practices such as *dhikr*; Jews to Kabbalah or to rabbis who delve into mystical Judaism; Christians to the burgeoning world of contemplative Christianity, where long-buried practices are being renewed.

- Give preference to methods with proven track records. The testimony of trusted friends can be a reliable source, but speak to other practitioners as well. Find out if any empirical studies have been done on the technique.

- Enquire about both immediate results and long-term benefits.

- Favor methods that feel natural and can be performed with ease on your own. No strain, all gain.

- Find an instructor with solid experience and certification from a reputable lineage or organization.

- Give peace a chance. Approach any new practice in the spirit of objective research. Do it as instructed and for long enough to be able to evaluate it properly. Look for tangible benefits in your life. That's where the proverbial rubber meets the road: not so much how you feel during meditation but whether the practice upgrades your walk through this crazy world. If, over time, you notice greater equanimity and clarity of mind under stress, more overall peace and happiness, deeper compassion toward others, and an elevated capacity for giving and receiving love . . . well, then you know you're really on to something.

CHAPTER 3

Before and After the Stillness

Practices to Frame Meditation

Know well what leads you forward and what holds you back, and choose the path that leads to wisdom.

— BUDDHA

There are an infinite number of spiritual paths, one for every person who seeks the Infinite. Your path may seem identical to someone else's, but at best it's similar. It's yours and only yours. That is as it should be and as it must be. As Swami Vivekananda said in a lecture in 1900, "We should never try to follow another's path for that is his way, not yours."

As the pilot, navigator, and captain of your spiritual ship, you get to decide what to practice and when. This book aims to give you plenty of options to choose from. In the previous chapter, we looked at meditation as a natural starting point, a foundation on which to construct a holistic spiritual routine. Here, we'll focus on techniques to use immediately before and after meditation. The before methods create optimal conditions for deeper meditation; they're preparation, like a singer's vocal warm-ups or a high jumper's running start. The postmeditation options smooth the transition back to active life. Some options will also add an element of devotion to your routine, if that suits your spiritual aspirations. Note that most of the techniques in this chapter can also be used as stand-alone practices.

PRELUDES TO MEDITATION

In 2019, a Harvard Medical School publication summarized the findings of a set of studies this way: "Available reviews of a wide range of yoga practices suggest they can reduce the impact of exaggerated stress responses and may be helpful for both anxiety and depression." It added, "By reducing perceived stress and anxiety, yoga appears to modulate stress response systems. This, in turn, decreases physiological arousal."[11]

---

[11] "Yoga for Anxiety and Depression," *Harvard Mental Health Letter*, originally published in April 2009 and updated May 9, 2018.

Note the term "wide range." Unfortunately, thanks to the incentives of commerce, the word Yoga has become synonymous with the stretches, bends, and postures depicted in magazines. This has reduced the entire Yoga tradition to a fitness regimen in the public mind. It's far more than that, of course. As we've seen, the larger purpose of Yoga techniques is to foster the liberated state of unified consciousness that is the very definition of Yoga. Toward that end, the physical postures called *asanas* that most Westerners value for their health benefits have been used for centuries as part of a sequence of practices. They're typically followed by breathing methods known as *pranayamas*. The combination reduces agitation, draws the senses inward, and settles the mind so meditation can begin from a deeper place.

Postures and Positions

The yogis who developed the catalog of asanas understood that the physical is a conduit to the nonphysical. Most spiritual traditions concur, hence followers are urged to treat the body as the temple of the soul—or, as Buddha called it, the "vehicle for awakening"—by keeping it strong and unpolluted. Doing asanas prior to meditation is analogous to running an antivirus program before working on your computer.

As important as asanas are for a holistic spiritual strategy, I can't in good conscience teach you how to do them in the space available in this book. It is too easy to injure yourself by misconstruing a written instruction or attempting a posture that is not right for your physical condition. I highly recommend finding a well-trained instructor and acquiring a sequence of easy-to-do asanas that suits your physiology and capabilities—and is safe to do on your own. If you prefer to learn from a book or video, please exercise caution.

When you do asanas at home, please bear the following in mind:

- Wear nonconstricting clothing and practice in a peaceful space where you are unlikely to be disturbed. Don't watch TV or listen to the news. If you want a musical accompaniment, make it relaxing, not stimulating.

- Use a yoga mat, preferably atop a carpet or blanket as opposed to a hard surface.

- Favor an easy, relaxing sequence. If you like vigorous, fitness-oriented Yoga, do it at other times rather than as a prelude to meditation.

- Consider having two or three routines to choose from depending on your physical condition and time constraints. Even a few minutes of gentle stretching can be highly rewarding.

- Do the exercises slowly and luxuriously, without exertion or strain.

- Keep your attention on your body; monitor the physical sensations and be alert to signs of discomfort.

- Never force yourself into a painful position; trying to imitate the pretzel postures in magazines is an invitation to injury.

- Don't try to bend or stretch beyond your capacity; just move toward the desired end position and stop when going further might cause pain or undue stress on your body.

- Remember, you are doing asanas not only for their health benefits but to refine the central nervous system so it is more receptive to deep spiritual experience.

Progressive Relaxation

If you are not inclined toward Yoga asanas, you might want to try a different practice to reduce physical tension before meditation. The traditional Chinese systems of chi gong and tai chi are good alternatives. Or perhaps you'd feel more comfortable with the progressive relaxation method of tensing and relaxing muscle groups sequentially. The following variation, which begins at the feet and moves up to the head, is both effective and easy to do—and it couldn't be more convenient.

Sit comfortably or lie on your back on a cushioned surface. Keep the lighting dim. Breathing in, tense the muscles in your feet and calves by pointing your toes toward your face. Hold that tension for 5 to 10 seconds. Now let go of the tension as you exhale. Relax for 5 to 10 seconds.

To tense and release the upper part of your lower legs, point your toes *away* and curl them downward as you inhale. Hold. Let go as you exhale. Relax.

Continue in this fashion progressively upward: tense as you inhale, hold, let go as you exhale, relax.

Tightly clench the muscles in the front of the thighs. And relax them.

Then the backs of the thighs.

The buttock muscles by squeezing the cheeks together.

The stomach muscles by pulling them in as if to form a tight knot.

The back by arching up and away from the surface you're resting on.

The chest muscles by holding the breath and pulling your arms tightly to your side.

The arms by clenching your fists tightly and flexing your biceps.

The shoulders by shrugging upward toward the ears.

The front of the neck by lowering your chin toward your chest.

The back of the neck by pressing the back of your head against the seat back or pillow.

The mouth, cheeks, and jaw in two ways: by pressing your lips together and clenching your teeth, and then (after relaxing) opening your mouth as wide as you can.

The eyes and nose by squeezing your eyes tightly shut.

The forehead by wrinkling it into a deep frown.

As you practice this sequential method, notice the profound difference between the state of tension and the state of relaxation. This will help you recognize muscular tension at other times so you can release it.

Respiration Inspiration

Isn't it interesting that the word *inspiration* applies not only to oxygen intake but to creativity, emotional upliftment, and religious epiphany? Since breath is the necessary condition for life itself, it's no wonder it's associated with life-enhancing things. Nor is it surprising that ancient seers and modern scientists alike have used systematic breathing to produce beneficial physical effects. The Yoga tradition made a virtual science of it, developing a vast collection of breathing exercises, some so easy a child can do them and others so demanding that only advanced yogis should even attempt them.

Yogic breathing falls under the rubric of *pranayama*. Like the Chinese word *chi,* the Sanskrit word *prana* is usually translated as "life force," referring to the subtle energy that is said to animate all lifeforms. *Pranayama* is typically translated as control of the life force. In practical terms, it applies to breathing practices with life-enhancing benefits.

As mentioned, pranayama is usually performed after asanas and before meditation, as a bridge between bodily movement and meditative stillness. Simply put, by quieting the breath, we quiet the mind.

Alternating Currents

By far the most common form of pranayama is alternate nostril breathing, a.k.a. *nadi suddhi*. It quickly brings calm to the mind and body and, it is said, enhances the coherence of the brain's two hemispheres. Here's a simple, easy way to practice it:

- Sit erect but comfortably. If you're going to transition directly from this breathing exercise to meditation, it's a good idea to sit in the same place for both.

- Close your eyes.

- Press the outside of your right nostril with the tip of your right thumb so the air passage is closed off.

- Breathe in through your left nostril— just a normal breath, perhaps slightly deeper than usual, but without strain.

- At the top of your breath, switch nostrils by releasing your thumb and closing the left nostril with the middle and ring fingers of your right hand. Now your right nostril is free.

- Breathe out at a normal pace through the right nostril.

- After exhaling completely, breathe in through the right nostril, keeping the left one closed.

- After the inhale, switch nostrils again. Release your fingers from the left and close the right with your thumb as before.

- Exhale completely through the left nostril.

- Breathe in deeply through the left nostril.

- Switch nostrils again.

- Continue in this manner: out, in, switch nostrils; out, in, switch nostrils; and so forth. Five minutes or so should suffice.

Once you get used to the practice and have done it for a while, you might want to try some variations to deepen the relaxation. For example:

- Hold your breath for two or three seconds at the completion of each inhale and exhale.

- Lengthen the in- and out-breaths. Take a full, deep breath, pushing out your abdomen like a balloon and filling your lungs completely. Hold. Then exhale completely, pulling in the abdomen to force all the stale air out of your lungs. Hold and continue.

- Adjust the in-out ratio. Research shows that elongating the exhale to about 50 percent longer than the inhale calms the body-mind quickly, tripping the switch from the fight-flight physiology to its opposite.[12] So, inhale slowly to a count of four; hold for a count of four; exhale to a count of *six*; hold for a count of four. Repeat and continue in that manner. In time, you may want to experiment with longer counts. But guard against straining; pranayama is a process of refinement and purification, not a contest.

---

[12] Technically, this is mediated by stimulating the vagus nerve, which turns off the sympathetic nervous system and activates the parasympathetic. Breathing in this ratio is beneficial anytime, not only during alternative nostril practice.

The Breath of Victory

Another technique that relaxes the body and steadies the mind is *ujjayi* breath.[13] The key to this practice is to slightly constrict the throat muscles when breathing. This narrows the passage through which air flows, creating a sound that's been compared to soft snoring, a hiss, the ocean tide, breathing through a tube, and Darth Vader. That sound is your barometer for knowing you're doing the technique correctly.

To get started, exhale through your mouth and make a "hah" sound, as if you were fogging a mirror. Now *inhale* through your open mouth and make the same sound. Got it? Now close your mouth and do the same thing, making the same sound while inhaling and exhaling through the nose. That's it.

This simple but powerful method can be used in a number of ways. It is mainly performed as an exercise of its own for a set period of time, inhaling and exhaling to a prescribed count or while intoning a mantra internally. Some Yoga teachers instruct students to breathe this way throughout asana practice, and it can be used as the method of breathing during alternate nostril and other pranayama methods. You can also practice ujjayi anytime you feel the need, adding an extra dimension to the impact of a few deep breaths.

---

[13]   It is pronounced "oo-jye" and translated as "victorious breath."

There are dozens of variations of asanas and pranayama. By all means, shop for the ones that suit you best. When using these variations for lmdlmgh s as meditation lead-ins, remember to do them gently, calmly, and utterly without stress and strain. They don't have to be done for very long. Ten or fifteen minutes of asana and five minutes of pranayama will usually suffice.

AFTER MEDITATION

In the previous chapter, I suggested taking some time to transition from meditation to active mode. That quiet postmeditative state is an ideal time for add-ons that suit your mood, circumstances, and spiritual orientation. Here are some suggestions.

Send Out a Prayer

Whether you believe in a personal God who hears and responds to human requests or an impersonal universe in which heartfelt thoughts have consequences, or that the brain can be reprogrammed by words and feelings, the postmeditation period, when the ego is likely to be held at bay, is a good time to pray.

How should you pray? In whatever manner suits your beliefs and your feelings at the time. Not only does the content of prayer vary widely, so do the intentions and expectations of those who pray and the depth at which they experience the process. Prayer can be robotic, routine, and insincere; it can also be profoundly transformative. Its purpose can range from extreme self-interest to complete self-surrender. It can be a petition for something you want, a desperate plea for a miraculous intervention, a request for guidance, an application for forgiveness, a compassionate appeal for the welfare of others, an offer to serve ("make me Your instrument"), or a proclamation of devotion, adoration, or thanksgiving from an overflowing heart. In every instance, launching a prayer from the runway of deep silence makes whatever power it may have that much greater.

However you may pray at other times, let your after-meditation prayer be uttered inwardly or in a soft whisper. You may want to recite a familiar prayer from a religious tradition, or you may be moved to improvise and let your feelings flow. Just do it with sincerity and humility, and remember the insight of the Danish theologian Søren Kierkegaard: "Prayer does not change God, but it changes him who prays."

Here are some prayers to consider in crazy times:

From Judaism: "Help us, O God, to lie down in peace and awaken us to life on the morrow. May we always be guided by your good counsel, and thus find shelter in Your tent of peace. . . . Guard us always and everywhere. Bless us with life and peace. Praise to You, O God of peace, whose love is always with us."

From Islam: "Guide us, O God, on the path of perfect harmony, the path of those whom You have blessed with the gifts of peace, joy, serenity and delight, the path of those who have not been brought down by anger, the path of those who have not been lost along the way."

From Christianity (St. Francis): "Lord, make me an instrument of your peace: where there is hatred, let me sow love; where there is injury, pardon; where there is doubt, faith; where there is despair, hope; where there is darkness, light; where there is sadness, joy."

From Hinduism: "Lead me from the unreal to the real, from darkness to light, from death to immortality."

From Buddhism: "May all beings be free of suffering. May all have happiness and contentment. May all be peaceful and at ease. May all be protected from harm and fear. May all be healed. May all awaken from their illusions and be enlightened. May all be free. May all beings abide in the great innate peace."

Or, if you prefer, the benediction often intoned a few times by yogis after completing their sadhana: *Lokah samastah sukhino bhavantu.* The usual translation is "May all beings in every realm be happy and free."

Then again, you could keep things utterly simple and follow the advice of the Medieval Christian mystic Meister Eckhart: "If the only prayer you ever say in your entire life is thank you, it will be enough."

Chanting Aloud

Similar to prayer but with the added element of musicality, intoning a chant can be an enlivening, even ecstatic transition from meditation. You could, of course, quietly sing a hymn or a sacred song that is meaningful to you. But intoning a chant in its original language adds the value of benign sound vibrations and reduces the cognitive interference of processing familiar English words. This is one reason traditional Sanskrit chanting, called *kirtan*, has become popular. The rhythmic repetition of mantras takes the benefit of singing to another level. Other traditions have similar rituals using Hebrew, Latin, Arabic, Farsi, and other venerable languages.

A common way to conclude a meditation session in India is to chant the mantra *om*. Now quite familiar thanks to its use in Yoga classes, the sylla ble is considered sacred because it is said to be the primordial sound of the cosmos. If you were able to step outside the universe, you would hear om emanating from it. When chanted, the sound does not rhyme with *home*. It's more like *aum* (and is often spelled that way). Hence, *AaaaaOoooMmmm.* Try chanting it aloud three times after meditation—and if you like it, chant it immediately *before* meditation as well.

If you'd like to try a traditional devotional mantra, this one is widely used throughout India: *Om Namah Shivaya.* It is usually translated "I bow to Lord Shiva," the name of the Hindu god of destruction. Modern gurus explain that Shiva is synonymous with Supreme Reality or Inner Self; hence, the mantra is a salutation to the boundless, indwelling Self of all selves.

Intone the mantra, rinse away stress, and repeat as needed.

If you're not comfortable with Sanskrit, or with deities associated with Hinduism, you might prefer this Buddhist chant (*gate* is pronounced "gah-tay"):

Gate gate para-gate para-sam-gate
Bodhi svaha
Gate gate para-gate para-sam-gate
Bodhi svaha
Gate gate para-gate para-sam-gate
Bodhi svaha

Translation: Gone, gone, gone utterly beyond the other shore. Awakening, hail.

Many Christians intone one of these Latin phrases:

Veni, Sancte Spiritus (Come, Holy Spirit)
Agnus Dei, qui tollis peccata mundi, miserere nobis (Lamb of God, who takes away the sins of the world, have mercy on us)

Meditating Jews might like to chant the Shema. Often called the most sacred recitation in the Jewish liturgy (from Deuteronomy 6:4), it is a declaration of divine Oneness: *Sh'ma Yisra'eil Adonai Eloheinu Adonai echad*. The usual translation is "Hear, O Israel, the Lord is our God, the Lord is One."

Not surprisingly, the Arabic *La Ilaha Illallah* is similar to the Shema in both meaning—"There is no god but God"—and the ecstatic effect when chanted in a group.

It's easy to find chants from various traditions online so you can hear the correct pronunciation and see samples of rhythms. A few repetitions are usually sufficient in this context.

Imagine That

Visualization is another common practice whose power is enhanced by a calm, settled mind. That makes it a good candidate for use after meditation. The power of imagination has been harnessed by spiritual traditions around the world. In recent times, visualization has been used to reprogram the mind everywhere from corporate sales training to psychotherapy to pregame locker rooms. The intent of the heart-opening visualization that follows is to spread the blessings you receive in meditation. You might want to make an audio recording of the instructions so you don't have to open your eyes to read during the practice.

Sit comfortably with your eyes closed. Imagine a ball of pure white light forming in the center of your chest. Consider this light radiant with divine love.

Abide in the supernal light for a moment or two, then allow it to spread in expanding arcs: upward to fill your chest, your rib cage, your shoulders, your neck, your chin and mouth, your nose, your eyes, your ears, your skull.

Bring your attention back to the source of light in the center of your chest. Now allow it to spread downward and outward to your arms and hands, your solar plexus, your stomach, your intestines, your pelvic region, your hips, thighs, knees, shins and calves, ankles, and feet.

Be still, and imagine the brilliant light filling every cell of your body. Feel its tender warmth and the unconditional love that is its essence.

Now transmit that healing light beyond the borders of your body to fill the room you're in. And further outward to fill the entire building. And further to heal the city. The state, province, or region. And the entire country.

Keep radiating that divine light outward from your heart. If you are in the United States, see it spread to all of North America (adapt for your location). Then to all of South America. Across the ocean to Europe. To Africa. To the Middle East. And all of Asia. Australia and New Zealand. The Pacific Islands. And the entire planet and all the beings in it.

Radiate further to encompass the moon. The sun. The solar system. The galaxy. And all the uncountable galaxies that speckle the heavens, until the light of love fills the entire universe.

Sit with this expansive love for a while. When you're ready, relocate to the present moment in time and your point in space, feel your body, and abide in the light for a couple of minutes before opening your eyes.

Sacred Study

The postmeditation state is a great time to open a sacred text and ponder a passage, a page, or a chapter. You may have had the experience of reading something you had read once before, at an earlier time in your life, and finding it so rich that it was as if you were reading it for the first time. Reading with a clear, calm mind, relatively unfettered by distraction and preconception, can be like that. So consider keeping a book—or a few of them to alternate—close to where you meditate. Read from beginning to end in increments, or open to random pages, or choose sections you find especially meaningful.

Read slowly and contemplatively. Don't rush as if you were doing a homework assignment. Sink into it. If you're so inclined, ponder the symbols and metaphors. Consider what the original intent of the scribes might have been. Self-reflect: What is the book telling you at that moment? How might this or that passage inform your own spiritual life?

Linger wherever you feel invited to. Absorb. Assimilate. And watch your reactions. Does a certain word or phrase stir your soul or make your heart skip a beat? Why? What does that reveal? You may not know the answer to that question, but an increment of wisdom has surely been added to your account.

Abide in Awareness

Whatever practices you engage in after meditation, when you're finished, it's a good idea not to just bounce out of your seat and plunge into action. Dwell in the silence a bit, doing nothing, intending nothing, expecting nothing, anticipating even less. Rest in the attitude described by the great Christian mystic Thomas Merton in *The Climate of Monastic Prayer*: "The true contemplative is not the one who prepares his mind for a particular message that he wants or expects to hear, but who remains empty because he knows that he can never expect or anticipate the word that will transform his darkness into light."

Just mind your Is-ness. Bathe in plain, unsweetened, unsalted Being. And in that minute or two of receptive abiding, perhaps something—an insight, a revelation, an answer, a message, a sign, an intuition, the word of God—will arise from the empty fullness and the full emptiness.

Or not.

Either way, you'll feel better than you did before. You will have spent time in your inner sanctuary. Some of the serenity you absorbed will stay with you. And you will radiate that peace outwardly, making this crazy world a little more sane.

CHAPTER 4

Spiritual Time Management

Filling Out Your Repertoire

The person who constantly studies without doing
spiritual practice is like the fool who attempts
to live in the blueprint of a house.

— MATA AMRITANANDAMAYI

You may have heard the old joke about the tourist in New York who asks a passerby, "How do you get to Carnegie Hall?"

The answer: "Practice, practice, practice."

That's also the answer to questions like "How can I stay grounded in this crazy world?" and "How can I make faster spiritual progress?" Practice is how we access our inner refuge. It's how we gain the strength and skill to stand up for what's right.

Practice, practice, practice. Doing that consistently requires commitment, proficient time management, and an ample supply of methods that match your changing spiritual needs and time constraints. This chapter aims to help you on all three counts.

INVESTMENT, NOT OBLIGATION

Back when I started meditating, if I told people I sat with my eyes closed for 20 minutes before breakfast, they'd react as if I began my day poking needles into a voodoo doll. Now I get letters from my health-care provider saying they offer meditation and Yoga classes. What used to be weird is now preventive medicine, so you would think that regular spiritual practice would be as common as stopping off at Starbucks for a caffeine fix. Instead, for a great many people, it's more like cutting down on carbs: they know it would be good for them, but they just don't get around to doing it.

Why don't they? The reason I hear most frequently is "I don't have the time." If you're one of those people, I suggest keeping a detailed record of everything you do and how long you do it over the course of a typical week. You may be shocked, as many have been, to discover a gap between your values and priorities and how you actually spend your time.

In my experience, people who truly appreciate the benefits of regular spiritual practice make the care and feeding of their souls a high priority. They find the time for it—if not an hour, then half an hour; if not half an hour, then 15 minutes; if not 15, then 10 or 5. If you're in the noncommittal camp, unsure if the investment of time is worth it, consider making a conditional commitment to a set of practices so you can see whether they bring concrete, unmistakable benefits to your life. If, after a reasonable period of time, the evidence is still murky, and you're not sure if the techniques have real value, here's a tip: get feedback from people who know you well. Ask if they see changes in you that you might not notice yourself. "You must be doing something right," they might say. "You used to hit the roof when such and such happened!" Or "You're in much a better mood lately. Are you on meds or something?" I've seen that gift of positive reinforcement bestowed many times; the people close to us see us in ways we cannot.

But most of the time, it's obvious. For more than 50 years now, I have rarely gone a full day without meditating. I know dozens of people like me, and they'll all tell you the same thing: They don't do

their sadhanas out of fear, or faith, or a sense of obligation. They do it for the same reason they do their
laundry and take showers and service their cars—
because it has demonstrable value. They have seen
clearly the difference in their lives when they've
practiced and when they haven't. I was lucky to discover that early on. The spiritual methods I adopted
proved to be radically transformative, and that data,
so to speak, was reaffirmed every step along the way.
My practices became precious to me in the most
tumultuous period of my life; they proved equally
precious when I was stable and happy; and they
remain precious now.

That said, I've been able to be consistent because
I'm also flexible. Committing to daily practice does
not mean getting locked into a rigid sequence or an
ironclad period of time for the rest of your life. We
can adapt to changing life conditions and spiritual
priorities. We can freshen things up in a thousand
ways, by adding new techniques, for instance, or
tweaking a method that may have grown stale. If
you bring to your path a spirit of ongoing learning
and curiosity, you will never lack new and valuable options.

The bottom line is this: once the value of ongoing
practice has been personally verified, the purported
obstacles dissipate. It stops being seen as a luxury

item, or a superfluous pastime, or something for the bucket list. Instead, it is cherished as a blessing or appreciated as a long-risk investment that yields substantial short- and long-term returns in well-being and performance enhancement.

Consider Mahatma Gandhi. He did not have to commute to an office or shuttle kids to soccer practice. But he was rather busy trying to drive a colonial power out of his homeland and reconcile factions in the independence movement. At the start of one especially busy day, Gandhi is said to have remarked, "I have so much to accomplish today that I must meditate for two hours instead of one."

Meditate on that for a while.

MAKING THE TIME

I know you have the motivation and the time for spiritual practice. How do I know? Because you were drawn to the title of this book and you've found the time to read this far into it.

If you choose effective practices that suit your needs and personality, fitting them into your day will not be that difficult. You'll find time for them, just as you find time for other useful or life-enhancing things, even if it means shedding some time-wasters or cutting back on second-rate pastimes. Maybe you get up a little earlier and go to sleep that much sooner. Maybe you cut back on social media. Maybe you take a break at work, shut the door, and put your mobile devices on airplane mode. Maybe you spend part of your lunch break on a meditation cushion, or on a yoga mat, or in a nearby church, or under a tree. Maybe you do a practice in your office at the end of the day and head home a bit later. Maybe you do a walking practice on the way home or a sitting practice on the train instead of reading news reports that might only make you nuts.

If it's really hard to figure out a way to squeeze a practice period into your busy life, consider whether you have too much on your plate to begin with. Is everything you spend time on necessary? Can you remove any clutter from your days? Reexamining your priorities can, in itself, be a spiritual discipline.

Over time, regular practice will strengthen your spiritual immune system and fortify your inner sanctuary. But let's be honest. In these maddening, tension-packed times, a daily routine is not always enough. Sometimes, we crave additional healing, rejuvenation, and nourishment to keep the wolves of fear and despair from entering our stronghold. We need a booster shot of inner peace to counter the incessant clamor. We need an extra dose of Spirit to restore our souls and realign our motives with the Good. And, when dark energies assault us, we need to discern whether the right response is "Don't just stand there, do something!" or the opposite: "Don't just do something; stand—or sit—there."

We're action-oriented. When we see a problem, we want to fix it. When we see a menace, we instinctively dive into the fray. That's the famous fight-or-flight response, the essential survival mechanism that enabled our ancestors to slay the wild beast that invaded their settlement or to gather their children and flee to safety. That reflex is still being triggered today even though, for most of us, our current threats seldom require physical mobilization. The well-documented result of activating our physiological alarm system is anxiety, imbalance, fatigue, and a plethora of stress-related illnesses.

A different kind of survival logic sometimes dictates the need to interrupt that fight-flight reflex and activate what has been dubbed the "rest-and-digest" response. This is the logic of maintenance, of rejuvenation, of neutralization. It's a rational shift from fighting or fleeing to taking shelter, regrouping, and gathering reinforcements. It's stepping back from the battle to sharpen your spear. It's climbing to higher ground to enlarge your perspective.

There are times when we have to remember that wisdom. We have to trust the intuition that tells us to retreat when our bodies are mobilizing for action. I learned about this decades ago when the early research on stress made it to the mainstream press. I've written about it and helped others understand it. And still I forget. Even as I write this very chapter, part of me says, "Stop working. Get away from your computer for a while," as another voice argues back, "Shut up, lazybones, you have a deadline. There's no time for some silly 'spiritual break.' You have to finish advising readers to take a spiritual break."

After all these years, I am much better at recognizing when it's time to put my nervous system into airplane mode, so to speak. And yet part of me will sometimes resist, and I need the kind of help I'm doling out here.

The material we turn to now, and add to in subsequent chapters, will help you navigate the rocky shoals of our crazy times when your daily spiritual routine needs reinforcement.

YOUR SPIRITUAL INVENTORY

To supplement your regular spiritual practices—and to modify them when appropriate—it's helpful to have an ample collection you can draw from to meet your needs and circumstances in any given moment. To accomplish that, I recommend stocking up on effective methods for nourishing the mind, healing the body, and elevating the soul. And to make your repertoire accessible and applicable as your life conditions change, I suggest organizing the practices around a range of time frames. For example:

- Less than 5 minutes.
- 5 to 15 minutes.
- 15 to 30 minutes.
- A half-hour to an hour.
- 1 to 3 hours.
- A full day.
- One day to a week.
- A week to a month.
- More than a month.

Feel free to modify these time slots as you see fit. The idea is to create a handy reference source, both for planning ahead and for immediate use when you feel a spiritual tug and need a practice that hits the spot. Bear in mind that some practices can be entered in more than one category since they can be done for different lengths of time. "Take a walk," for example, can mean five minutes in the corridors of your office building, or half an hour around the neighborhood, or two hours in a park. (I recommend including specifics like those in the appropriate time category.) Obviously, the same applies to other time-flexible practices as well. You can do one Yoga asana for 30 seconds or spend an hour on a comprehensive sequence, and similar options exist for prayer, reading scripture, service work, and many other practices.

You'll find that you include many more items in the shorter time frames than the longer ones. For obvious reasons, you'll also draw on the briefer practices more frequently. The spacious end of the time spectrum is meant for special events that typically require thinking ahead: a sacred pilgrimage, a bucket-list vacation, a reunion with precious people, a spiritual retreat. Some activities, of course, can range in duration from days to months. In the one-day category, for example, you might include your version of a Sabbath—what Rabbi Abraham Joshua Heschel called "a sanctuary in time"—whether you schedule one on a weekly basis, as some religions prescribe, or shut down on occasion for a day of quiet reflection.

Your lists in the shorter time frames will grow faster than you might expect. You'll be surprised, for example, how many spiritually fruitful things you can do in just a few minutes. Music breaks, for example, you might create a spiritual playlist for use in the under-five-minutes section, entering a range of selections to suit different moods and conditions. Such a playlist can get quite long, especially if you reach beyond what's normally considered "spiritual" music, like hymns and chants. Why not sanctify other genres by including songs that move you deeply or make your spirit soar? Sometimes, a pop tune may be exactly what you need, whether it's Billie or Beyoncé, Sinatra or Sheeran.

In fact, your under-five section might get so long you end up breaking it into narrower categories. How about "under a minute"? How long does it take to take a deep nasal breath and forcefully exhale through your mouth? How long does it take to text a heart emoji to a loved one? How many seconds does it take to read a psalm, a profound sentence from a sacred text, or a stanza from Emily Dickinson or William Blake?

The methods described in previous chapters can be entered into your inventory, of course, and you'll find more to add later in the book. But you'll want to stretch further. Why not sample the goods in the bounteous spiritual marketplace? Both online and in person, you'll find a cornucopia of useful practices.

I also suggest sifting through your memory bank for activities that once ignited a sacred spark in you or that in some way soothed your troubled soul. Bring friends into the process and share ideas with one another.

And tune in to your internal Spiritual Positioning System. We all have one. Call it an SPS—or maybe a Spoogle because it's like a spiritual search engine. It's preprogrammed for spiritually beneficial destinations, and it automatically knows your location on the sacred path. You may have already programmed it with a wish list: workshops, seminars, and classes you've thought of enrolling in; meditative practices you've wanted to try; retreat centers you've been hoping to go to; that cabin in the woods you almost rented for a long weekend; the sacred journey you've always dreamed about; the church/temple/mosque you've been meaning to attend. Once you know how to access it, your SPS will communicate through your intuition and route you to the most appropriate practices.

Err on the side of inclusion; you never know when something that doesn't particularly excite you now might be just right sometime in the future. Include devotional rituals, mental disciplines, physical techniques, solitary practices and communal ones, acts of receiving and acts of offering. And don't restrict yourself to the usual suspects. Expand the definition of "spiritual." What takes your mind off the world's turmoil and your personal troubles? What lifts and frees? Which amusements? Which people? Maybe feeding pigeons in a park does it for you. Watching a goofy comedy. A drive in the country. Which places have you longed to discover or return to? Which books have you wanted to read? Which loved ones and inspiring friends do you not see often enough?

While inclusion and expansiveness are desirable, try not to settle for mere diversions, and beware of enticing escapes that might have unwanted side effects like injury, or fatigue, or relationship stress. Favor activities that are likely to culminate in greater joy, contentment, love, and mind-expanding, soul-enriching knowledge. Constantly reprogram your SPS for what your spirit yearns for.

ADDENDUMS AND CAVEATS

As you fill in your inventory of practices and begin to draw from it, keep these points in mind:

- You are the decider. Advice is good. Guidance is essential. But only you can decide what to practice and when and for how long. Evaluate each practice honestly, applying both rigorous discernment and intuitive perception. Keep the ones that produce benefit and discard those that don't—or set them aside for a later time when they might prove useful.

- Avoid spiritual promiscuity. Adding to your inventory through ongoing exploration and experimentation is vital, but beware the risk of becoming a dilettante. Spiritual dabblers have been compared to a person who keeps digging wells in search of water but never digs deep enough to find any. They've also been likened to a hungry person at a buffet who grabs a bite of everything that looks good but never gets properly nourished. The lesson: by all means try on practices for size, but wear them long enough to break them in and see if they really fit. Endless sampling can be just as counterproductive as a stubborn commitment to a practice with limited value.

- Monitor yourself. It's easy to find excuses for slacking off on spiritual practice. "I'm too stressed out." Really?

What better reason to unlock your inner sanctuary? "I don't need it, I feel great." Congratulations, but saving spiritual practice for moments of dire need is like taking target practice only on the battlefield. I also hear "I need a more comfortable place" and "It's too noisy." Think of the yogis doing their sadhanas on the forest floor and the monks and nuns on hard benches in frigid cells. If you can't enhance your comfort or find a quieter place, make the discomfort part of your practice. Consider this parable: The head monk is on his deathbed. The other monks gather around him to receive final instructions. One of them asks, "Master, what should we do about the crazy man from the village who barges in and bangs his drum when we're meditating?" The Master smiles and says, "Keep paying him."

- Find your balance. Diligence is good. So is persistence. And consistency. What's *not* so good? Fanaticism. Extremism. Obsession. Overzealousness. Don't meditate enough? Not good. Meditate too much? Also not good. The spiritual path has been called a razor's edge and a narrow ridge. When traversing such a precarious route, you need balance. Lean too far in either direction, and you're asking for trouble. That's why every wisdom tradition counsels moderation. Having seen the futility of excessive austerity, Buddha created a safe path to nirvana and called it the Middle Way. Locate your point of balance, and keep the adage attributed to Ralph Waldo Emerson in mind: "Moderation in all things, including moderation."[14]

• Lighten up. "Angels can fly because they take themselves lightly," said the British author G. K. Chesterton in his 1908 book *Orthodoxy*. If you're overly earnest about spiritual practice you can suck all the joy out of life, and how spiritual is that? I've seen people get so spiritually rigid that they make a mess of their relationships and careers. I've seen others wallow in guilt because they compromised on their practices. Enjoying life can be a spiritual act. Laughing at your own foibles can be sublime. So give yourself a break.

---

[14] It has also been attributed to Oscar Wilde and Mark Twain.

- Right intent. Anything can be spiritualized. Conversely, what in profound in the sacred can be vulgarized. As someone once said, "Sitting in a church doesn't make you spiritual, just as sitting in a garage doesn't make you a car." Eating, for example, can be a matter of filling your belly with anything edible—or a sacrament in which every bite is a prayer of thanksgiving. Sex can be a selfish act of gratification—or a sacred rite. Helping your neighbor can be a transactional obligation—or a compassionate act of service. The right attitude can make the mundane holy, and that, in itself, is a spiritual practice.

CHAPTER 5

Changing Your Mind

Working with Perception, Framing, and Attitude

The mind is its own place, and in itself
Can make a Heaven of Hell, a Hell of Heaven.

— JOHN MILTON

On the morning I started work on this chapter, I woke up early, showered, and did my usual morning practices. Afterward, I turned on the news to see what was going on while I dressed and brewed a pot of tea. Big mistake. In my face was coverage of the aftermath of mass murders in El Paso and Dayton, shouting matches over gun control, and ominous portents in the trade war with China. Then a bulletin: sex trafficker Jeffrey Epstein committed suicide in prison, denying his victims their day in court.

My inner peace shattered like broken glass. Noting the linguistic link between bulletin and bullet, I could feel stress hormones surge through my body as rage and sorrow tumbled around in my chest like a toxic cocktail mix.

I shut off the TV and poured a cup of tea. My inner cynic teased me: "Hey, you've only been meditating half a century. That equanimity you wrote about must need more time."

Upon reflection, I realized that what I said in previous chapters does hold up. I stabilized quickly, recovered my perspective, and soon had enough of that prized equanimity to write a coherent draft of these sentences you're reading. None of which would have been possible without my commitment to spiritual practices.

But I also realized this, and not for the first time: it's not enough.

Especially in crazy times, we might need more than a daily sadhana and an assortment of supplementary practices. We need immediate remedies, tools for damage repair, and weapons for fighting back. In the next few chapters, we'll add to our toolboxes. In this one we'll focus on the mind and our perceptual apparatus—the stuff that's often disparaged as "in the head" but has a lot to offer the heart and the soul.

MINDING THE MIND

"Everything can be taken from a man but one thing," wrote the Austrian psychologist and Holocaust survivor Viktor Frankl in *Man's Search for Meaning*: "the last of the human freedoms—to choose one's attitude in any given set of circumstances, to choose one's own way."

Frankl's famous statement is a lesson for the ages—literally the ages, as his insight has echoes in every era and every place. No matter what's going on, no matter how uncontrollable the events that assail us, we're in charge of our mental posture. This perennial insight went viral in 2008, thanks to Harvard neuroscientist Jill Bolte Taylor. Following a massive stroke that left her cognitively impaired for several years, she wrote a book called *My Stroke of Insight* in 2006 and two years later delivered a hugely popular TED talk about what she'd learned from her ordeal. "I may not be in total control of what happens to my life," she said in her book, "but I certainly am in charge of how I choose to perceive my experience."

Do you doubt that? It's easy to understand why, because it seems as though thoughts and feelings arise as if launched by some automatic software operation. But while we can't always prevent rubbish from littering our minds, once it arrives, we can keep it from piling up—and maybe replace it with a nice flowering plant.

The Swinging Doors of Perception

Reflect for a moment on the shifts of attitude, mood, and perception you experience on a daily basis. Notice how they change for no apparent reason. Something that annoys the hell out of you on one occasion seems trivial, maybe even funny, on another. Events that trigger fear or anxiety might, the next time, seem perfectly tolerable and relatively harmless. For example, your child has a temper tantrum. Your heart swells. You reach out to comfort the adorable angel. Next day, the same child has the same kind of tantrum, only now you're in a rotten mood. You haven't slept enough. You're stressed over something at work. Your spouse ticked you off. Now how do you react? I know, it's painful even to think about it. In the first instance, nothing blocked your big-hearted Mommy or Daddy View. The next time? You saw a brat who was driving you nuts.

I often take walks on the beach in Los Angeles. Some days my heart swells in gratitude. On days when I'm preoccupied, worried, or angry, I may as well be on a treadmill in a dingy gym. Same surf, same sand, same sky. What's different? My inner state. And the reason it's different is not always easy to figure out.

ʏᴏᴜ ɢᴏᴛ ᴛʜᴇ ᴘᴏɪɴᴛ: ᴘᴇʀᴄᴇᴘᴛɪᴏɴ ᴍᴀᴛᴛᴇʀs, ɪɴᴛᴇʀᴘʀᴇ- tation matters; attitude matters; mood matters. And all those things are subject to change, depending on our mental habits and the whirling conditions of our minds and bodies. So here's a key question: Do you cede control of those shifts to propagandists, advertisers, entertainers, and random events, or do you take charge? You can't always control your circumstances, of course, but you *can* change the way you perceive and evaluate them.

The Big Picture

Most of the time, we view reality from the ground floor. In fact, sometimes it's as if we were standing on our tiptoes, peeking out the basement window. But if we ascend to higher levels, the vista expands at every landing. We see new things, and we see their interaction in a more spacious context. That's why armies post sentinels in towers.

The spiritual view is the equivalent of higher ground. When we shift mentally to the Big Picture, awareness expands, the heart opens, and the soul is liberated. Where do you find higher ground in difficult times? Perhaps it's in your religious faith, in phrases such as "It is God's will" or "We are in God's hands." Maybe you're drawn to one of the aphorisms commonly attributed to the Hebrew Bible even though they can't be found there: "The Lord moves in mysterious ways, His wonders to perform," or "This too shall pass"—the latter being almost Buddhist in affirming the impermanence of all phenomena. Perhaps you resonate with the assurance of the 14th-century Christian mystic Julian of Norwich, "All shall be well, and all shall be well, and all manner of thing shall be well," or Teresa of Ávila's advice, "Let nothing disturb you. / Let nothing dismay you. / All things pass. / God never changes."

Similarly, many people find it effective, when stuck seeing reality in a negative light, to shift to a saint's-eye perspective. "I ask myself, How would Buddha see this person who's making me mad?" a Buddhist practitioner told me. Others, of course, do the same with Jesus or another spiritual luminary. We can never know how the venerated masters would actually view the people and circumstances of our lives, but asking the question can only lift us up.

Perhaps you're like many spiritual voyagers who locate higher ground in the Eastern concept of karma, which posits a system of cosmic justice that sounds less like theology than like a scientific principle or a law of nature, like gravity. You've heard it expressed in colloquial terms, such as: every action has an equal and opposite reaction; we reap what we sow; what goes around comes around. In the Big Picture of karma, everything is right as it is, and justice prevails. In the long run, good is rewarded and wrong is penalized, even though it may not seem that way through our ordinary lens.

If you prefer a scientific perspective, the vastness of the known universe might do the trick. Check out the images from the Hubble telescope and contemplate the fact that what you're seeing actually occurred a hundred million years ago. Think about the worrisome present as the movement of a speck of dust in that limitless cosmos. Or maybe the historical view does it for you. History offers some evidence for Martin Luther King Jr.'s optimistic statement that "the arc of the moral universe is long, but it bends toward justice." Scholars have shown that our common feeling that things have never been worse is inaccurate. By many important measures, human life around the globe has been a lot worse at times, as the poverty, illiteracy, and spectacular carnage of the 20th century alone suggests. You can take that perspective a step further if you wish by entertaining the possibility that the turmoil of the present might be a sign of cleansing, like the discomfort that arises when the body rids itself of toxins. That theory could be dismissed as New Age drivel, but what if we *are*, as W. B. Yeats put it, slouching toward Bethlehem to be born?

If you find comfort in any expansive perspective, why not go there? Step into your mental elevator and press the button for Cosmic Penthouse.

But don't trick yourself into believing what you don't believe. Religious precepts and philosophical premises can lift your gaze and give you solace, but if, deep down, you think they're BS, they'll just be short-lived tranquilizers with possible bad side effects.

If you're an honest, inquisitive person, doubt might creep in. Karma sounds great, for example, but good people suffer and bad people thrive all the time. It's not unreasonable to think, *If it takes lifetimes for karmic law to work everything out, I'm not sure I can get on board.* Similarly, it's sensible to think, *"This too shall pass" is undoubtedly true, but look at the wreckage that's piling up while it's passing. When climate change finally passes, what will be left?* As for "God's will," you'd be in good company if you asked what kind of God we're talking about. Great minds have pondered for eons how all our suffering and misery is possible if the Almighty is really all-knowing, all-powerful, and supremely good. Something in that theology has to give.

If such thoughts arise when you're stepping up to higher ground, welcome them. Instead of suppressing your doubt or feeling guilty for having it, use it as an opportunity to question, reflect, and deepen your path. As Alfred, Lord Tennyson, said in verse, "There lives more faith in honest doubt, / Believe me, than in half the creeds."

An honest engagement with doubt might strengthen your trust in a familiar Big Picture, or it could move you to a different one, and/or it might propel you to a radically new transformational space: the path of unknowing. Welcoming, embracing, and rejoicing in the eternal mysteries can offer a surprisingly plush sanctuary. Call it the Yogi Berra School of Wisdom. When asked if he knows anything, the legendary ballplayer said, "I don't even suspect anything." It's a position of profound certainty of your own uncertainty, and it can lead to awe and wonder, surrender and humility—and maybe to a deep bow to the infinite Intelligence that runs the show. It can also prompt you to open your arms to the ineffable and laugh your head off over the magnificent absurdity of trying to figure it out. What a relief!

There is no contradiction in embracing the unknowable and at the same time having faith in religious or philosophical precepts. In fact, it's traditionally encouraged. The Bhagavad Gita asserts that the laws of karma are inviolable, yet it also says that the *details*—the precise causes and consequences of events—are so mind-bogglingly complex as to be unfathomable to the human mind. We are advised not to even speculate about the hows and whens and whys of karma. Ditto Western notions of God's will. Check out the book of Job, where the Almighty tells Job in no uncertain terms that the answers to his probing questions are utterly incomprehensible to humans. Dwell in the Big Picture of unknowing a while, and you might end up with Job (and Arjuna in the Gita), on your knees before the Divine Mystery.

Lifting your mind to your version of a cosmic view is an antidote to anxiety, anger, and other afflictions of our crazy world. Perhaps you remember the moment of collective revelation when, in 1968, all of humanity saw the image called Earthrise taken from the Apollo 8 spacecraft. In that and subsequent astronaut photos, the boundaries and divisions that wreak so much havoc were nowhere to be seen; the troublesome human beings were not even specks; the fierce urgency that distorts life on the planet dissolved into timelessness; and not a bomb, gunshot, sob, or scream could be heard.

FLIPPING THE MIND

Harding awareness to the big picture of cosmic harmony has an everyday equivalent: shifting the mind from negative to positive thoughts. Psychologists employ it under the rubric of cognitive behavioral therapy. Some call it reframing. It's been advocated in magazines and self-help manuals ever since the 1952 bestseller *The Power of Positive Thinking* and the even older musical ditty "Ac-Cent-Tchu-Ate the Positive."[15] In the Yoga tradition, it's called *pratipaksha bhavana*. The basic idea is, to replace negative, harmful, or debilitating thoughts with their opposites: gloom and doom with optimism, hate with love, disdain with compassion, and so forth.

Karmically speaking, thoughts are vibrating energy forms that emanate outward. They impact our surroundings in expanding waves, and the positive and negative effects eventually boomerang back to us in reap-what-you-sow consequences. If that proposition is too esoteric for you, just consider your own experience. Surely you've seen how dark thoughts find expression in your speech, actions, and demeanor. What are you contributing to the world in those circumstances? How do others respond? What do they give back to you? Do fear, hatred, and rage

---

[15] The book was written by Norman Vincent Peale; the 1944 song was by Harold Arlen (music) and Johnny Mercer (lyrics).

help or hinder your decision-making? Do disdain and faultfinding nurture or harm your relationships?

Think of it in physical terms if you like. If every thought is reflected in brain activity, then the intensity, frequency, and content of your thoughts will affect your nervous system for better and for worse. Scientists have compared the effects of negative and positive thinking, and the results are as you might expect. Optimism, for instance, has been associated with a number of desirable outcomes, from reduced anxiety and depression to lower risk of dying from a major disease. Numerous studies have established that inner happiness produces success more than success produces happiness. And data show that cultivating gratitude improves well-being, health, relationships, resiliency, and even quality of sleep.

Changing mental channels provides relief in the moment and, over time, can upgrade the mind's default settings. The instructions could not be more simple: when you notice toxic, negative, harmful thoughts in your mind, replace them with positive, elevating, harmonious equivalents.

Sounds easy, right? But in practice, reversing the polarity of thought is nowhere near as straightforward as turning a magnet around. The skill can be learned, however, and habitual negativity can be unlearned. Here are some guidelines to keep in mind:

Observe your mind.

Most of us entertain more negativity than we think we do. Get in the habit of allowing the witness part of your awareness to watch your mind stuff. Make note of habitual patterns that might damage your well-being, inhibit your spiritual progress, or trigger detrimental behavior. Stay alert for the appearance of those unwanted thoughts, and substitute more beneficial content.

Find the right replacements.

In our highly charged political climate, I have spoken to many people who get consumed by anger and hatred toward certain politicians. They don't like that those negative thoughts disturb their inner peace and take up mental space that could be used for better purposes. But they find themselves haranguing public figures over and over again, mentally hurling the same tirades and making the same accusations. They know that their repetitious discharge affects the politicians about as much as an unpublished letter to the editor, but they find it hard to stop. "I know about pratipaksha bhavana," one of them told me, "but when I try to replace those negative patterns, I think, *What's the opposite of hate? Love.* So I'm supposed to love those people? Not even Jesus could pull off that trick."

She tried, but it felt so phony that she got queasy inside and gave up.

This leads to an important point: replacement thoughts have to be believable, and if they imply taking action, the actions have to be feasible. That's because your subconscious mind knows what you really feel, and it won't tolerate empty platitudes or artificial moods. Try installing "I love so-and-so" when you can't stand so-and-so, and your subconscious will have a good laugh. If you persist in trying to cover virulent thoughts in rose petals, you'll drive yourself crazy.

In finding a true and appropriate replacement thought, don't take the concept of "opposite" literally. Use your imagination. For example, since loving thoughts about someone you despise won't work, why not switch channels to someone you *do* love? Someone whose name or image will instantly soften your heart. You might notice an immediate energetic shift. The woman with the politician hatred came up with a different solution: she replaced the anger with compassionate thoughts about people she thought were being harmed by the politicians' policies. Similarly, an environmental activist I spoke to seethed with animosity toward climate change deniers. He couldn't realistically replace his disgust with acceptance or indifference. His solution was to shift to heartfelt concern for those who will suffer most as the planet heats up, and to appreciation for those who are working to mitigate the danger.

Another strategy is to shift from furious into moral indignation—a calmer, less destructive form of disapproval that can also be a launching pad for intelligent action. Instead of "I'm pissed about such and such," it becomes "Such and such is wrong, and I want to do something about it." A Buddhist friend told me he tries to emulate the Dalai Lama, who said that his greatest teacher was Mao Zedong, the Chinese leader who invaded Tibet and drove the Dalai Lama into exile. "When I find myself hating on someone," my friend said, "I mentally thank them for the opportunity to learn something about myself, or about life."

We can work in a similar way with other common intruders. Take fear and worry, for example. They can be useful survival mechanisms, alerting us to potential threats. They can also cause harm by triggering the fight-flight response unnecessarily or excessively. If the fear and worry are rooted in actual reality, trying to replace them with some la-di-da, "it's all good" flimflam would be worthless. A more realistic approach—and therefore a more effective one—would be to shift from fear ("I'm terrified by this") to thoughts that reflect the feeling of concern ("This is a troubling situation that needs attention"). Concern is calmer than fear. It's more compassion-centered. It makes us attentive and open to solutions, whereas excessive fear can distort perception and rattle the mind.

As for worry, well, if you can do something about the situation, shift to a solution-oriented thought: "I'm going to solve this by ____" You can also supplement the verbal input with images of yourself taking feasible, constructive action. In this way, you replace worry with confidence and turn problems into challenges. What if there's nothing you can possibly do about the situation that worries you? Well then, worrying about it is useless, isn't it? In that case, one option would be to replace the worry program with a stated intent to limit the damage and protect your spiritual integrity regardless of what might happen.

The strategy for shifting mental energy in a more harmonious, uplifting direction, then, is to replace negativity with positive, appropriate alternatives that are both believable and true. Replacing harmful mind stuff with the energetic opposite restores balance and fosters spiritually beneficial feelings such as love, compassion, and gratitude.

No strain, no pain.

The attempt to substitute one thought pattern for another does not require strenuous effort. Begin by inwardly declaring your intent to curtail the negativity.

That alone can begin to shift the energy. Then politely *invite* the replacement thoughts or images to enter the ┈┈┈┈┈ ┈┈┈┈┈┈ ┈┈┈┈┈ ┈┈┈┈ ┈┈┈┈┈ ┈┈┈┈┈┈

Sometimes, spiritually denigrating thoughts erupt in an emotion-charged frenzy. Disturbing phrases and visual scenarios run through the mind over and over again like the proverbial hamster on a wheel. Introducing a favorable replacement under such turbulent conditions can be as hard as stopping a car when it's skidding on ice. You might be tempted to use force. You'd be wise to resist that impulse because the effort is likely to be futile, and you'll only end up more frustrated. This is a good time to call on a one- or two-minute practice from your inventory to lower the heat. Some deep breathing might do the trick.

Alternatively, detach your attention from the mental tumult, and place it on your body. Because thoughts and emotions have physical correlates, you'll notice sensations of different kinds. Just feel them. It might seem like forever, but the physical turmoil will usually subside rather quickly, and the mind will also start to settle down. Now, like an athletic coach during a time-out, you can call in substitutes off the bench.

Be patient.

Don't think you're a failure if you can't just sweep away unwanted thoughts like dust with a broom. Instead, praise yourself for being aware enough to know the harm such thoughts can bring and for having the spiritual dedication to do something about your mental habits.

It takes time to cultivate new skills. Our brains store the remnants of impressions, wounds, and traumas (yogis call them *samskaras*), and when negative traces of the past get triggered by new experiences, toxic thoughts can be launched. You'll want to banish them, but they might resist. Don't be discouraged. The ability to notice harmful patterns as they take shape in the mind improves with practice, as does the skill of replacing them. Eventually, it becomes more like a habit than a method you have to apply.

Grievance to Gratitude

In a sense, gratitude is the ultimate thought replacement. Like a baseball player who can handle every position on the field, gratitude can be summoned any time harmful mind stuff disturbs your peace and you need to restore order. It has a proven track record, too, with endorsements from sages and prophets, psychotherapists and neuroscientists.

Numerous studies have shown that gratitude produces major upticks in various measures of well-being. Research also showed that the grateful attitude can be cultivated. The simplest practice is to regularly set aside a few moments to write down things you're grateful for. How many items should you list? How frequently should you do this? There are no hard-and-fast rules. You might want to start by writing down one thing you're grateful for every night before going to sleep—or first thing in the morning for an upbeat start to your day. If that's too easy, write down three. Or five. You'll be surprised how many items come to mind once you invite them in. You might also be surprised by how much better you feel after realizing how much you're thankful for.

Some people find gratitude breaks so rewarding that they set a timer to beep at fixed intervals, signaling it's time to write down something they appreciate. Others find that even a once-a-day gratitude session is too much like a chore or an empty ritual. This virtually guarantees they'll stop doing it, so for them, once a week is probably better.

You might also try this variation: write down the things you're grateful for on small slips of paper, and deposit them in a jar. After a while, you'll be able to pick out an item at random whenever you need a gratitude pick-me-up.

Be aware that faked gratitude doesn't work. Studies indicate that you actually have to feel it to reap the rewards. Coming up with things you're truly grateful for might seem difficult at times, especially if you're trying not to repeat yourself too much. But if you're open to the process and pay attention to your life minute by minute, you'll find that you're surrounded by blessings. While we weep over the suffering caused by tragedies like floods, fires, droughts, political crackdowns, and mass murders, we can also bow in gratitude to the first responders and selfless volunteers who rise to the occasion. While raging against tyrants and despots, we can also sing the praises of the courageous dissidents who oppose them and the intrepid journalists who expose them. No matter what aggravates you, if you shift your attention, you'll find something to be grateful for: your health, your family, the view outside your window, the food in your refrigerator, the roof over your head, the hot running water, the rain, the paved streets, your very ability to think and feel, your spiritual practices, the people whom you love and who love you—and all the sources of friendly support we turn to in the next chapter.

CHAPTER 6

A Little Help from Our Friends

Taking Refuge in Relationship

I am because we are. We are because I am.

—SOUTH AFRICAN PROVERB

If you remember the late 1960s and early '70s, or heard about the era from your elders, you know that times have been crazy before, and in some ways crazier. As Vietnam burned and the military draft hung like a heavy stone on the necks of young men, as revered leaders were shot and cities erupted in riots, as the Watergate scandal grew more intense and mind-blowing, America was as divisive and jittery as it is today. Like many in my generation, I was fed up, infuriated, and worried about the future—mine and my country's. But it felt different then. Not just because I was younger, and not just because cable news, the Internet, and smartphones didn't exist. The main reason I experienced the turmoil differently back then is that I was part of a spiritual community.

My fellow travelers and I were in the world but at the same time spiritually removed. We worked together, ate together, played together, studied together, mated with one another, and shared information and concerns on a regular basis. Spiritual practice was a top priority, reinforced by collective agreement. For me, the question of skipping sadhana rarely came up, even though my routine was about three times as long as what I do now. Our conversations, regardless of topic, seldom strayed far from a spiritual perspective. We had signposts. We had guardrails. We had soul protection.

I eventually pulled away from that community when I came to feel the urge to explore beyond its narrow confines. But I've often missed its warm embrace.

We are, each of us, captain of our own spiritual ship. But the ship is not a kayak; it's a vessel on a sacred voyage, with a large scope and a precious cargo. It may sound paradoxical, but on the spiritual path, we are on our own—and we can't do it alone.

We are independent and also dependent. Personal freedom is crucial, and so is companionship. Mapmakers, navigators, and brother and sister voyagers are indispensable.

ORGANIZED COMMUNITIES

For many reasons—overwhelming schedules, the gig economy, people moving from place to place, dependency on social media—community has become harder to come by. But organized spiritual communities can still be found, and the human connection they afford can be much more rewarding than the virtual versions.

Dedicated Buddhists vow to take refuge in the traditional "three jewels": Buddha, which does not necessarily refer to the historic person but to one's own "Buddha-nature"; Dharma, defined in this context as "the path" or "the teachings"; and Sangha, the community of aspirants. In fact, every tradition assigns great importance to fellowship. The Abrahamic traditions prioritize the congregational bonds of church, mosque, and synagogue. A famous passage in Hinduism's ancient Rig Veda includes this entreaty: "Come, let us be together. . . . Let us meet together, let us talk together, let our spirits grow toward union together." [16]

Spiritual togetherness offers not only refuge in difficult times but ongoing guidance, common rituals, shared theological and moral teachings, the opportunity for dialogue, and a sense of belonging. Like a packaged tour, spiritual groups can make the journey safer, more comfortable, more focused and orderly. In crazy times, it's one good answer to "Who you gonna call?"

If being part of a spiritual community appeals to you, ask yourself what *kind* of affiliation would best serve you. A homogeneous group with people who share your religious background and/or belief system? A diverse one, such as an interfaith or interspiritual organization? Would a formal organization with established gathering times, rituals, and celebrations meet your needs? Or are you more attracted to a loose, informal community, such as those developing around Yoga studios and meditation centers? Are you interested in a congregation linked to an alternative tradition such as New Thought (e.g., Unity Church and Centers for Spiritual Living)?

If you live in a metropolitan area, you'll find lots of options. Chances are you know people who have some involvement with various groups. If you accept

---

[16] Rig Veda, Mandala 10, sloka 12, stanza 40.

an invitation to check one out, don't be surprised if you're urged to come more often, or even to make a commitment. Take your time. Yes, it's risky to hop from group to group like a romantic adventurer who doesn't date the same person twice. But premature dedication to a new spiritual home can be just as hazardous. If you commit to an inappropriate relationship, you could be in bigger trouble than if you'd remained on your own.

Which brings us to the inevitable caveats. Spiritual community can be a haven, but also an obstacle course. It's both liberating and binding. It's a paradise with pitfalls. Even in a spiritualized context—maybe *especially* in a spiritualized context—groups are as imperfect as the humans they comprise.

I've researched many spiritual communities, and I've never found one whose members did not report some kind of dysfunction—sometimes with affection and humor and sometimes with bitterness. While packaged tours have much to offer, they can also be disappointing, inhibiting, and restrictive. Stuff happens. Personalities collide. Bureaucracies become stale. Leaders become autocratic. The saintly soul you admired turns out to be a phony. The sense of belonging that felt so cozy begins to feel oppressive.

Or not. Someone else's prison may be your utopia. You may strike gold, and there's plenty of it in them thar hills.

Keep the ambiguities of spiritual community in mind, and approach companionship in the spirit of Rumi: "Live at the empty heart of paradox. I'll dance with you there, cheek to cheek." And if you start to get disillusioned with a once-promising community, before you up and leave, ask yourself some questions, such as: Was I expecting too much? Am I being unreasonable? Am I mistaking ordinary human frailties for fatal flaws in this particular community? Am I doing enough to make it better?

Choose Your Orbit

Affiliations do not have to be all-or-nothing propositions. While many people sustain membership in a group for life, others move on to new associations or affiliate with more than one. Some steer clear of organizations altogether. And many stay put but change their level of commitment or the nature of their participation.

Most spiritual organizations resemble the classic image of an atom, with a nucleus where the greatest power resides—in the pastor, the guru, the leadership council, etc.—and circles orbiting at different distances around the nucleus. The closer you get to the center, the more spiritual energy is usually found and more benefits can be obtained—and more is demanded by way of loyalty, commitment, and conformity.

The key is to reflect deeply about what you want and need from a spiritual institution and evaluate whether those wants and needs can be met by the one you're in. It's also important to assess both the risks and rewards of involvement and to determine if the balm of belonging may have side effects. Here are some questions to ask yourself:

- Am I able to be myself in that community?
- Can I speak my mind honestly without fear of ostracism?
- Are topics that matter to me treated as taboo?
- Are doubt and disagreement tolerated?
- Do any policies offend my values or ethics?
- Are the leaders arrogant? Self-important? Contemptuous of other institutions?
- Is there too much pressure to conform?
- Am I getting what I need and want spiritually?

Whatever you do, don't expect perfection. It doesn't exist. If you decide to leave or participate less, don't throw out the baby with the bathwater. Hold on to the good stuff. Even sanctuaries with leaks in the roof can provide some refuge.

BYO Sangha

Not everyone is the joining type. If you're not comfortable in an institutional community, why not create your own group?

All it takes is to gather some like-minded friends to meet on a regular basis. Start with a few people you're comfortable with. Meet in someone's living room or a conference room in an office building or library. When you're ready to expand, put out the word in an agreed-upon manner. Based on my own experience with small spiritual groups, here are some issues you and your initial companions may want to clarify at the outset:

- What is the main purpose? Is it to be a study group focused on shared readings or videos? A discussion group centered around issues of importance to the members? A practice-oriented group in which the bulk of your time is spent doing spiritual exercises? Is it primarily a support group stressing emotional comfort and help with spiritual challenges? Or is it some combination of the above?

- Is it homogeneous or heterogeneous? How diverse do you want the group to be, in terms of spiritual orientation, age, political beliefs, and other criteria? Will you draw from one tradition or explore a broad spectrum?

- How much structure? Should every session follow the same format? Or should the procedures vary depending on the circumstances? Do you want to establish regular rituals?

- What are the rules? Can the members agree to guidelines they think will best serve their purpose? Do they chafe at the very idea of rules? Think, for example, about whether confidentiality should be a ruling tenet. Decide whether members can speak at any time or if you prefer an orderly procedure, such as using a talking stick.

- What about governance? How will decisions be made? Should meetings be facilitated or leaderless? If facilitated, should the same person always lead, or should that role rotate among members?

- How often will you meet? Weekly? Every other week? Monthly?

- How many members do you want? Too few, and meetings get stagnant or repetitive; too many, and you might lack intimacy and coherence. How will you decide whether to invite new members? If you do open up, how should the newcomers be selected?

- How will you deal with conflicts? Don't assume your merry band of sweethearts will never argue, irritate one another, or break down in factions over some contentious issue. You might want to discuss how to handle disruptions right from the get-go.

- Are political issues off the table or part of the agenda? This is no trivial matter in today's heated atmosphere. You may want to avoid charged topics altogether and focus exclusively on spirituality. On the other hand, helping one another cope with our divisive times may be a prime reason for coming together. If you do discuss controversial issues, should there be standards of behavior? Limits on how long people can rant? Rules for expressing disagreement respectfully? Who enforces the standards? Think carefully about these things; I will never forget the pain of having a group I valued fall apart over the Iraq War.

Lectio Divina

If you and your spiritual companions are drawn to the shared reading of sacred texts, consider using the traditional practice of *lectio divina* (divine reading). Created by early Catholic monks, the practice has been used in different forms for centuries by people of all faiths as a method for deepening scriptural study. Here are instructions (adapt them for individual use if you're practicing alone):

Have the group or a designated member select a short passage from a scripture or another source you find inspiring and rich in meaning.

One member of the group reads the passage aloud, slowly and deliberately. The others either listen receptively or read along silently.

Repeat that step, only this time each person pays attention to their inner reaction to the content being read and notes which word or phrase leaps out.

Silently, each person mentally repeats that word or phrase several times.

Then go around the room and have everyone speak aloud the word or phrase that called to them—without explanation or commentary.

Now the reader repeats the entire passage aloud. Each member attends to their inner reaction, noting whether the feeling around their word or phrase has changed or taken on new meaning.

Take some time for everyone to contemplate their experience. This silent period can be limited to a few minutes or extended for as long as the group feels is suitable.

Each person briefly shares their experience with the group, describing what the entire passage or their specific word or phrase means to them.

Close with a period of meditation and/or some kind of invocation.

The group might want to make some ground rules for lectio divina. For example, setting a maximum time for each sharing (to avoid extended monologues), barring unsolicited advice, or pledging that everything shared will be held in strict confidence.

Spiritual Buddies

Even if you belong to a valued spiritual group, you might benefit from another, more intimate level of companionship. In ancient China, the swords some warriors carried were so long they could not be unsheathed while strapped to the waist. So the warriors traveled in pairs and, in times of urgency, drew one another's swords. Spiritual buddies can provide that kind of support.

That's why the informal community of friends, family, and others is indispensable. People you trust and respect, with whom you share history and mutual concern, can add solace, support, and wisdom to your path. They can help you locate your inner strength, resiliency, and courage when you most need those qualities. They can offer insight into yourself and help you glean useful lessons from life's ups and downs. They can supply resources and information. Fresh perspectives can be invaluable in puncturing our illusions and challenging our assumptions. And, perhaps most important of all, true friends hold us accountable. We all slip and slide. We slack off. We get sidetracked. We struggle with doubt and disillusionment. We get stuck in indecision. Like the sponsor for a person in recovery, a true spiritual companion will help keep you on track.

Are there dear ones in your life who can be elevated to a higher level of spiritual intimacy? Can you make your exchanges with them more open, honest, and enriching? Are there soul mates you don't see often enough? Can you schedule lunches? Take walks together? Use Skype or Zoom? We all know that social media can be major time-wasters, but they can also facilitate contact with people who matter. Why not upgrade your digital friendships and stand shoulder to shoulder in cyberspace as well as in the flesh?

That said, a thousand emojis can't match one compassionate nod, one appreciative gaze, one tender pat on the shoulder, and especially one big, warm hug. It's worth making the effort to connect in person.

Wheat and Chaff

One valid and crucial way to protect your spiritual sanity in these days of intense feelings and obnoxious trolling is to be discerning about your companions. Who creates drama and distress, and who gives you refuge? Who are the peacemakers, and who the troublemakers? Sometimes it makes sense to shed the sources of aggravation, especially if you've made an honest effort to relate to them in a humane way.

Nevertheless, we need all the help we can get in crazy times, so it might be wise to err on the side of inclusion. It's only natural to seek the company of people who think as we do. We derive strength and hope from "We're in this together." But consider this: maybe there is something extra to be gained from the difficult people, the ones with whom we don't see eye to eye and who sometimes irritate and frustrate us. You can't throw everyone overboard as briskly as you block people online. They might be relatives or co-workers or even—OMG!—people you live with. Can you use those interactions to tap into something spiritually beneficial?

Maybe you can make some proverbial lemonade out of astringent relationships. Try seeing them as teachers, as the Dalai Lama did with his Chinese tormentors. Can you welcome annoying people as facilitators of your curriculum in this life? Difficult relationships can strengthen our spiritual skills, just as exercise strengthens our muscles. They present opportunities to practice spiritual attributes we all want more of: forgiveness, compassion, love, empathy, acceptance, understanding. Sometimes it's not easy to bring forth those traits even with people we care about. But we usually do it. Can you also rise to the occasion with those you consider fools and spiritual pests?

If you're up to it, ask yourself if you're being too judgmental. Do you habitually find fault instead of looking for signs of goodness? Can you transform your disdain into a kinder feeling? Remember, you'll be doing it not for the other person, but to protect your soul from toxic emotions.

Give and Take

Relationships are a testing ground for the axiom that it's more blessed to give than to receive. Among your spiritual companions are people who need from you the kind of love, sympathy, and help you hope to get from them. You can give it even if you don't think you're up to the task—in fact, maybe *because* you think that.

The opportunity to give of yourself is what makes spiritual companionship a practice, not just a refuge. Why not take advantage of it? Giving more than we can hope to receive is not just a good moral principle, it's good karma. If it helps, think of it in practical, transactional terms: giving copiously pays dividends. The more you exhibit spiritually generous qualities, the more you attract the same. Give comfort and you will be comforted. Teach and you will be taught. Love and you will be loved. Help others cope with the crazy world and they will help you cope.

Spiritual Authority

One subgroup of spiritual companionship deserves special attention: authority figures. Priests and ministers, imams and rabbis, gurus and swamis, roshis and lamas—we need their guidance, their knowledge, their expertise. They know things we don't. They've had training we haven't. They might also have uncommon kindness and be willing to serve as confidants and mentors. At their best, they point the way to the light.

Having a trusted spiritual authority figure to turn to in crazy times is a blessing. But here come the inevitable caveats. Tibetans compared gurus to fire: if you stay too far away, you won't get the warmth; if you get too close, you can get burned. In other words, if you don't trust a good spiritual teacher enough, you lose out on vital knowledge and spiritual direction; but if you trust the wrong person too much, you can run into trouble. So if you crave wisdom, find a truly wise teacher. If you need spiritual guidance, choose a skilled and compassionate counselor. If all a person can offer is religious platitudes and spiritual clichés, you probably want to look elsewhere. And if you have more acute psychological needs, such as beating depression or healing old traumas, make sure you find either a spiritual leader with the proper skill set or a professional therapist who understands your spiritual leanings.

Relationships with spiritual teachers are not unlike marriages: when the match is good, there is no greater blessing; but when the parties are not well matched, what should be a sacred support system becomes a dysfunctional mess. Also like a marriage, a student-teacher relationship can suffer from inflated expectations. Holding teachers to high standards is vital, but it's also important to be realistic. Finding an appropriate spiritual guide requires both discernment and humility. "Before taking someone as a teacher, be careful. Use your critical faculty and subject that teacher to scrutiny." No less an authority than the Dalai Lama said that. Don't let a title, institutional status, or saintly demeanor make you trust a person blindly. Don't put anyone on a pedestal, either, and if you come across a teacher who's already on a pedestal, be especially vigilant. They're all human. Projecting godly perfection or infallibility onto them does a disservice to both student and teacher.

Determine in advance which roles you most want a teacher to play. Trusted advisor? Learned friend? Expert instructor? Master? Commander? Counselor? Mentor? Beloved? Identify the types of relationship that best fit your needs. And never relinquish your own power. The best spiritual teachers empower the sage within you.

OUT-OF-THIS-WORLD FRIENDS

Spiritual companions don't have to be present in the flesh. The saints and sages of the past can serve as exemplars of the highest ideals and role models to emulate. If, for example, you need a model of grace under fire, think of Jesus, Gandhi, Martin Luther King Jr., and others who confronted powerful forces while grounded in Spirit. We've all heard of Christians asking, "What would Jesus do?" Well, Buddhists do the same with the historical Buddha. Hindus reference Lord Krishna and the noble characters in their epics, the Ramayana and the Mahabharata. Muslims, of course, look to Muhammad and the revered figures who succeeded the Prophet. Jews can turn to a generous assortment of biblical characters, from Queen Esther to Moses.

For those so inclined, the great ones of the past are not just exemplary figures but divine presences with whom to communicate. So too are various deities, angels, and other nonhuman beings. Certain types of prayer are designed precisely for that kind of give-and-take. Skeptics might sneer at such practices, but they can be effective for the faithful, and even for those who believe the response to prayer comes from their own inner voice and not a disembodied entity. Why not try it when you need some comfort or guidance? Immediately following meditation might be a good time for a static-free reception.

Of course, if you're devotionally inclined, the ultimate spiritual friend is God, however you imagine Him or Her or It. Why not enter into a dialogue? It's not everyone's cup of tea, but it can be powerful if it suits your personality and belief system. Reverence is the proper stance in an I-Thou dialogue with the Almighty, but censorship is not required, so don't hold back. Express your worries, your fears, your doubts— even, or especially, if you have doubts about God's very existence. Are you pissed at the Creator of a world with inexplicable cruelties? Shout out your rage. Let it all hang out, and when you've finished venting, quiet down. Convert your feelings into questions, and humbly present them. Then wait and listen.

Connecting with Unseen Guides

Some people find guided meditation an effective way to receive comfort and wisdom, whether they believe it comes from within themselves or from an actual being. Here is a practice you can adapt as you wish. I recommend reading the instructions into a recording device, slowly and softly. By playing back the audio, you won't have to open your eyes to read or rely on memory. If you find soothing music helpful, by all means play some in the background.

Lower the lights. Sit or lie down comfortably. Close your eyes.

Take three deep breaths, exhaling completely after each. Notice the soothing calm as your mind and body settle down. Invite each part of your body to relax even deeper.

Now visualize yourself embarking on a journey of peace, love, and truth. See yourself walking on a path through a serene woodland setting. Take in the beauty of the wildflowers and the shafts of sunlight slanting through the trees. Enjoy the natural scent of the forest, the touch of the breeze, and the sounds of birds chirping.

You come to a clearing. There you see a beautiful golden dome. It radiates pure light from within its walls. It is a holy place. It beckons you with the promise of healing and revelation.

Your intellect may tell you it's just imagination, but your heart knows this sanctuary really exists, at the core of your being.

You approach a magnificent door. You open it. You enter. A luminous space welcomes you. A seat awaits you in the center of the room. You sit. A feeling of peace comes over you. Your worries and resentments dissolve.

A hazy figure appears before you. You are filled with awe and reverence. As the being approaches, it comes into focus. It might be a deity or an angel. It might be an embodiment of the Almighty. It might be a beloved holy person from history or someone you've known who represents the highest of human qualities. It might be a persona you create in the moment. Or it might be no discernible figure at all, but a radiant orb of holy light representing the transcendent, formless Absolute.

Whatever shape it takes on, it embodies unconditional love, pure compassion, and divine truth.

The figure speaks to you. The voice is gentle and strong. It says, "I know who you are. I love who you are. I know the pain you've endured. I know what you yearn for. Your journey begins anew right here, right now."

Allow yourself some time to absorb that message. Notice how it feels to take it in. The voice continues:

"I ask only that you open your mind to the omniscient intelligence of the cosmos. That you open your body to the healing power of nature. That you open your heart to the limitless love of the Infinite. That you open your soul to Oneness."

You bow in gratitude. Wordlessly, the form before you invites you to ask any question you may have. What do you long to know? What mystery do you want solved? Take your time, knowing that you will have other opportunities like this.

When you know what you want to ask, have your imagined persona articulate the question.

Remain there in silence, basking in the presence of all that is sacred, good, and pure. The reply may come immediately or at a later time. In either case, know that it springs from the deepest place within you.

The figure blesses you. It begins to dissolve into pure light. And slowly it fades away.

You stand and leave the domed sanctuary, knowing you can return at any time. You are at peace, empowered to take your next steps boldly and courageously.

Now return your attention to the present moment, in this room, in this body. Gently stretch, or rub any part of the body that needs attention. When you're ready, open your eyes and resume your life.

If you find this exercise of value, repeat it any time you feel the need. Note that the answers that arise from your wisdom source may surprise you. They might be crystal clear on one occasion and enigmatic on another. You might have to probe for their deepest meaning. At times you might receive no discernible answer at all, in which case ask yourself if that might be the very answer you need. As Father Thomas Keating said in *Invitation to Love*, "Silence is God's first language; everything else is a poor translation."[17]

---

[17] A similar quote has been attributed to Rumi: "Silence is the language of God, all else is poor translation."

CHAPTER 7

Shelter from the Storm

Finding Safe Harbor in Sacred Spaces

Your sacred space is where you can find yourself again and again.

— JOSEPH CAMPBELL

On April 15, 2019, as I was preparing my tax return, I received a text with a frowning emoji and the words "Notre Dame." I turned on the news to see Paris's great cathedral burning. As I watched the spire collapse and the red flames engulf the roof, I became surprisingly emotional. My reaction was odd because I'm not Catholic and I've been to Paris three times in my entire life for a total of 15 or 16 days. Yet I felt heartbroken, as if my former home was aflame.

I later realized that I was lamenting the loss of a sacred space, and sacred spaces are vital habitats for the soul. This is especially true in stormy times, when we need safe harbor. So, in this chapter, we'll discuss how to extract the most value from places of refuge—and how to create your own, whether out in the world or in the safety of your home.

HOLY OF HOLIES

In my few visits to Paris, I spent many hours in and around Notre Dame, gazing at the structure from all angles at different times of day and night. I always felt elevated by its magnificence. Exquisite architecture can evoke awe and transcendence every bit as much as a mountain range or a field of wildflowers. But Notre Dame is not just a breathtaking work of art. It is a container of holy vibrations. Within its thick walls, millions have prayed, poured out their hearts in love and anguish, and offered up their souls. You could feel that energy whether you were sitting in silent meditation or having your bones rocked by the mighty organ. The fire was especially tragic because repositories of divine energy are precious.

If you have access to a public space with the same mix of aesthetic and spiritual splendor, you are fortunate. If you don't, you have many other options. When I lived in New York City, I would often find respite in an open church or synagogue in whatever neighborhood I happened to be in. You too can find such sanctuaries. You don't have to believe a word of the theology that's preached in the place. And of course you're by no means restricted to houses of worship. You might be well served by a library, especially if you value books like writer Anne Lamott, who said, in *Plan B: Further Thoughts on Faith*, "Libraries are like mountains or meadows or creeks: sacred space." A park bench can be sacred space. So can a puddle-sized pond, a pier, an empty ball field, a quiet museum gallery, an unused room in an office building, a hospital chapel, or a lonesome tree.

When you think about it, *every* space is sacred space. How can it be otherwise when omnipresent Divinity is . . . well, present everywhere? The Infinite is not holding back and waiting to reveal Itself. It's right here, ready for you to snap out of your slumber and recognize it. "This place where you are right now, God circled on a map for you," wrote the Persian mystic poet Hafiz.

Hafiz would have enjoyed a nice walk with the novelist J. D. Salinger, who had one of his characters say: "All we do our whole lives is go from one little piece of Holy Ground to the next."[18] This place is Holy. That spot is Holy. Every object, every form, every inch of space is Holy.

Ah, but before we run off thinking that one place is as good a spiritual refuge as another, a quick reality check. Oxygen is everywhere, but it's easier to breathe deeply in some places than others. Similarly, Divine Presence is everywhere, but it is, to most of us mortals, more discernible and more palpable in some places than in others. Let's face it, a Las Vegas casino and a Buddhist temple feel quite different, and while you might perceive Divinity in the former—after hitting a jackpot perhaps—your odds are decidedly better in the latter. If you were placed in a room, blindfolded with your ears plugged, and asked if you were in a police station or a monastery, you'd probably answer correctly.

Another, even more important caveat: the sanctity of a place depends largely on the sanctity you bring to it. Wherever you are may be Holy Ground, but holiness is in the heart of the beholder. "God resides wherever we let God in," said a Hasidic rabbi. If you're sufficiently receptive, the Divine will reveal itself in surprising places, even in a kitchen, which is where the 17th-century monk Brother Lawrence famously found it: "In the noise and clatter of my

---

[18] From the novella *Seymour: An Introduction.*

kitchen, while several persons are calling for different things, I possess God in as great tranquility as if I were upon my knees at the blessed sacrament."

Of course, for most of us, kitchens are just places to cook. We need places where the sacred is more easily accessed. Which ones work for you? Identify your favorite sanctuaries, and write down visits to them in your inventory of spiritual practices. Go to them often. Sit. Look. Feel. Breathe. Be fully present. Open yourself up to what is being transmitted. And be grateful.

MOTHER NATURE'S CHILD

If man-made sacred spaces are like saunas that pull toxins from the soul, immersion in nature is like a spa vacation. In a famous passage from his essay *Nature*, Ralph Waldo Emerson wrote about being in the woods: "There I feel that nothing can befall me in life,—no disgrace, no calamity, (leaving me my eyes,) which nature cannot repair. Standing on the bare ground,—my head bathed by the blithe air, and uplifted into infinite space,—all mean egotism vanishes. I become a transparent eye-ball; I am nothing; I see all; the currents of the Universal Being circulate through me; I am part or particle of God."

We don't all have Emerson's celestial perception, but we can at least approximate it, and we can place ourselves as often as possible in nature's cathedrals. Few places are as purifying as an unspoiled landscape, where the colors come straight from the Creator's easel, where the sounds are the same songs hummed by Earth's first fauna, and the air comes straight from green oxygen factories.

Whether you access nature in the woods, on beaches, or in city parks, treat every opportunity as a sacrament. Just be there. No agenda, no expectations, no earphones. Try to bring to every moment the power of your full attention. When you look, really see; when you listen, really hear; when you sniff, really smell; when you touch, really feel. "When we are mindful, deeply in touch with the present moment," Thich Nhat Hanh tells us in *The Long Road Turns to Joy*, "our understanding of what is going on deepens, and we begin to be filled with acceptance, joy, peace, and love."

Slow Down, You Move Too Fast

For the purpose of finding sanctuary in nature, haste really does make waste. A leisurely, contemplative walk will usually be more spiritually fruitful than huffing and puffing. If you're accustomed to an energetic jog or a hike, by all means enjoy your workout, but at some point slow down and linger. You can refine your stroll using various methods, such as:

- Attend to the senses. Feel the rise of your foot and the heel-to-toe touch as you step, then feel the lift of the other foot, its swing forward, and its contact with the ground. Notice the variety of shapes and colors around you; take in the scents; hear the sounds of rustling leaves and the singing of birds.

- Follow your breath. You don't need to consciously change your breathing patterns; just breathe through your nose and focus on the feel of the air as it enters your nostrils and fills your lungs . . . and then on the release of the breath as it exits your chest and nose . . . and on the automatic re-intake portion of the breath cycle.

- Coordinate breath and footsteps. If you're not self-conscious about walking ve-e-e-ry slowly where other people might see you, synchronize the step of one foot with the duration of your natural inhale and the other foot to the out-breath. If that slo-mo walk is uncomfortable, try syncing the steps of

both feet with the in- and out-breaths.
Find the step-and-breath combination
that works best for your natural pace—
nothing artificial or contrived, just a
natural rhythm.

• Chant or pray. Especially if you find
your mind drifting off into banal
or unpleasant trains of thought, try
coordinating your steps to the internal
chant of a mantra, or the rhythm of
a favorite hymn, prayer, psalm, or
poem. Or improvise your own lyrics of
gratitude to the melody of breath and
the beat of your footsteps.

Such mindful walking is not limited to ambles
in nature, of course. It can be applied when march-
ing to the subway or parking lot, in the supermar-
ket aisles, at the shopping mall, in the corridors of
a building . . . in short, any time you're ambulating
through space.

Take a Stand, or a Seat

When you're in a natural sanctuary, try to be sta-
tionary for five minutes or longer. Be still and know,
as in the familiar Bible verse, "Be still, and know that

I am God."[19] Know that this—wherever you are—is hallowed ground. Know that you are blessed to be there. Know that whatever else is going on in the world—whatever horror, whatever suffering, whatever dismal portents—you have this sacred moment in this sacred space. And you can carry home some of its beneficent gifts like priceless souvenirs.

Once you're settled in, shift your attention from the whole to the part. Focus on one object. "The ideal of man is to see God in everything," Swami Vivekananda once said. "But if you cannot see Him in everything, see Him in one thing, in that thing which you like best, and then see Him in another. So on you can go."

A tree would be a great choice. Trees are not only beautiful, awesomely complex, and givers of shade and fruit, but studies suggest that their very presence—even in winter, when the branches are bare, and even on a city street—can have a beneficial effect on measures such as anxiety, fatigue, depression, hostility, blood pressure, stress hormones, and fear. One study suggests that trees may even lower the crime rate in the surrounding area.

Look at the tree. Examine its parts. Watch the branches sway and the leaves dance to the music of the wind. Spy on the birds taking a breather on the

---

[19]   Psalms 46:10.

branches, and the squirrels and insects ascending and descending the trunk. If your mind wants to engage, contemplate the intricate anatomy of the tree and its interdependence with everything around it. Reflect on the orderly miracle of leaves dying and being reborn.

Go ahead, hug the tree. No one is watching . . . and if they are, tell them they don't know what they're missing. Thank the tree for comforting you with its presence and for vacuuming up the carbon dioxide. And hey, if you really feel grateful, why not channel that feeling into a contribution to the greater good? Plant a tree. Not only will it help mitigate climate change, but one day someone might sit before the tree you plant and find refuge from the crazy world.

If the whole tree seems too big and complex to focus on, narrow your gaze to one of its parts—a branch, a leaf, the bark, the roots gripping the earth. Or choose another object—a bush, a flower, a stem, a stone, or a handful of dirt. Whatever you focus on, do it in the spirit of this passage from the great Russian novelist Feodor Dostoyevsky: "Love every leaf, every ray of God's light. Love the animals, love the plants, love everything. If you love everything, you will perceive the divine mystery in things. Once you perceive it, you will begin to comprehend it better every day. And you will come at last to love the whole world with an all-embracing love."[20]

One more point about being in nature. Just as an indoor sanctuary doesn't have to be Notre Dame, an outdoor one needn't be Yosemite or a beach in the Bahamas. It can be anywhere there's a patch of green or a source of water.[21]

Okay, one *more* point: don't limit your excursions to daytime. Head out of town, away from the city lights, preferably to a loftier altitude, and gaze in wonder at the night sky. "Let your soul stand cool and composed before a million universes," as Walt Whitman put it in "Song of Myself." As you stare at the inconceivable vastness of billions upon billions of galaxies, the emotion that might come over you, if you let it, is awe. And there's nothing like awe to make the concerns that ruin our days seem fleeting and small. Contemplate the fact that you are part of something inexpressibly magnificent and inconceivably vast. Ponder the possibility that this wondrous moment was arranged just for you . . . and, at the same time, you are just one insignificant speck among an infinite number of specks on an incomprehensible time-space continuum.

---

[20] From *The Brothers Karamazov.*

[21] For good ideas about being in nature, see Micha Mortali's book *Rewilding: Meditations, Practices, and Skills for Awakening in Nature.*

While you're at it, contemplate this stanza from a Rainer Maria Rilke poem:

> *a billion stars go spinning through the night,*
> *blazing high above your head.*
> *But in you is the present that*
> *will be, when all the stars are dead.*

AWESOME ART

To soothe the soul, art does not have to be explicitly "spiritual" like the Buddha statues that steered me toward a spiritual path, or the Sistine Chapel, or a Madonna and Child painting, or the statues of Lord Shiva as the Cosmic Dancer creating and destroying the universe. It doesn't have to represent *anything*, for that matter; for proof, gaze for a while at a Kandinsky or a Rothko. For me, it can be Matisse or Monet or Jackson Pollock. For you, it might be Rembrandt, van Gogh, or Georgia O'Keeffe. Great works of art spring from the place where the soul meets the hands and emptiness takes on form. When you commune deeply with a masterpiece, you partake of that transcendent moment of creation.

If you live in a city with an art museum, take full advantage of it. It doesn't have to be the Louvre or the National Gallery. I've had moving museum experiences in Portland, Oregon, and Portland, Maine. Try to go when it's least crowded, and if a particular piece lifts your spirit, give it the time you need to soak it in fully.

The same principles apply to the sanctuaries of literature, music, and cinema. Identify works that soothe and uplift you, but don't ignore the spiritually transformative power of stories and songs that tear open your heart and make you empathize with the suffering of others, or that expand your awareness of life on the planet or make you feel grateful for the simple things or restore your faith and optimism. And by no means underestimate works that make you laugh at the absurdity of it all—or just let you escape the madness for a while. The profoundly spiritual poems of Gerard Manley Hopkins, Emily Dickinson, and Mary Oliver are temples of words, and Walt Whitman illuminates the mystical magic in ordinary things, but sometimes the wild and woolly Dylan Thomas or Allen Ginsberg might do it for you—or a bawdy limerick, or Dr. Seuss, or Ogden Nash's wordplay. *The Wizard of Oz* is always redemptive, but so is *The Godfather* if you watch it with the right frame of mind.[22] At times, Bach in your headset can be a godsend; at other times, you might seek refuge in Jay-Z or Springsteen. Sometimes, in fact, a sad

---

[22] For suggestions about movies whose spiritual value is not obvious, see the archive of reviews at www.spiritualityandpractice.com.

song can be as spiritually elevating as a Gregorian chant or a gospel tune. Music that expresses how you actually feel can be more healing than music that expresses how you *want* to feel. It's like being heard by a super-empathic friend, and the friend is a great artist. If you're going through a hard time, for example, try listening to Mavis Staples sing "Hard Times Come Again No More."

Some works of art transport and transcend by virtue of their content. Others take you into the heart of darkness, forcing you to experience human cruelty and depravity—and that too can be spiritual if it awakens moral indignation and compassion. Some artists plunge into the dark side to reveal the goodness and courage of those who combat it. Even what seems to be sheer escapism, like superhero fantasies or science fiction, can be emancipating; by stretching the imagination, they can help us imagine solutions to problems and alternative ways of being. And sometimes the art itself, regardless of its content, opens us to the Light through its sheer beauty and the genius of its execution. Let it work on you.

While we're in an artsy mood, let's not forget a form of refuge that works on another level entirely: *doing* art. Draw. Paint. Write a poem. Sign up for the ceramics class or the piano lessons you've always wanted to take. Don't even consider whether anyone will like what you create. This is not about mastery; it's about getting out of your head. Nothing is closer to Divinity than egoless creativity, and the timeless joy of being "in the flow."

No time to take lessons? Don't want to spend money on a musical instrument? No room to set up an easel? Fine. Step right up to forms of creative expression that require nothing more than what's on hand. Drumming, for example. You don't need a drum kit and sticks. You don't even need a conga or a bongo; you can drum on a table, a stack of books, or the side of a suitcase. How about drawing? For that you need only paper and a pen or pencil or a box of crayons. Photography used to be an expensive art form, but now you have a camera and editing equipment in your pocket. And dance! No lessons, choreographers, or partners needed. Just turn on some music and boogie, as they say, like no one's watching—because no one is.

Above all, sing. Singing is not only the oldest art form, it's the most easily accessible. So make like Aretha and Pavarotti in the privacy of your home. You can also join voices with others, of course. The blending of souls in song is a multiplier; group consciousness magnifies the benefits. Let loose with the choir at a house of worship; join the call-and-response kirtan at a Yoga studio; start an a cappella group. If you have a voice, you can sing, even if you don't think you can.

SANCTIFY YOUR HOME

Franz Kafka, the celebrated writer from what is now the Czech Republic, is virtually synonymous with absurd, nightmarish stories. But he also wrote this unforgettable passage of spiritual advice, in a short piece titled "Senses": "You need not leave your room. Remain sitting at your table and listen. You need not even listen, simply wait. You need not even wait, just learn to become quiet, and still, and solitary. The world will freely offer itself to you to be unmasked. It has no choice; it will roll in ecstasy at your feet."

Just as you have a sanctuary within you, you have sacred space around you, in your own home. Like most of us, you probably cherish your home as a dwelling, but not necessarily as an abode of Divinity. If thinking of it in that way is too much of a stretch for you, consider sanctifying *pieces* of your home. Is it possible to turn a spare room, or a portion of a room, into a temple of sorts? If you can do that, ask yourself questions such as: What would make it as soothing, healing, and spiritually elevating as possible? What color might the walls be? Should I leave the walls bare or hang pictures? What about curtains? Floor covering? Lighting? Consider the seating, comfy chairs or meditation cushions? Should the space be austere or contain meaningful artifacts and religious symbols?

You might also want to create an altar. Altars can sanctify a room or grace a shelf, a tabletop, a counter, or a bureau. Place on it objects that evoke the highest thoughts and most tender feelings: photos of spiritual luminaries, sacred symbols, amulets, meaningful trinkets, photos of loved ones, or perhaps an indoor plant.

An altar can alter you. Don't just set it up and treat it like any other piece of furniture. Tend to it. Keep it clean. Renew it with fresh flowers and/or a change of artifacts from time to time. Treat it as you would a niche in a house of worship. Sit before it. Gaze at it as if seeing the objects for the first time. Bring to it your deepest concerns. Bask in the holy love it exemplifies.

You can situate miniature altars throughout your home. A picture, a small statue, a beloved symbol, and other objects can be placed strategically wherever your eyes are likely to fall as you go about your business. You might not register them much of the time, but when you do take notice, they may just lift your soul a little—and that's a lot.

Now here's a radical thought, inspired by Ram Dass, the late spiritual teacher who once had been Dr. Richard Alpert, Timothy Leary's fellow LSD outlaw in the '60s. During America's disastrous war in Iraq, Ram Dass was so disturbed by his anger toward George W. Bush that he placed a picture of the President on his altar. That incongruous presence alongside images of his guru and other revered figures forced him to remember that everyone is an offspring of the Eternal One. He continued to keep images of people he despised on his altar. "It reminds me of how far I have to go to see the Beloved in everybody," he said. And yes, he added a photo of Donald Trump in 2016.

Finally, consider bringing green life into your home sanctuary. Not only are plants soothing, but tending to them can be an act of devotion if you put your heart into it. And if you have space outside to create a small garden, it can be a private Eden, where the cycles of birth, death, and regeneration connect you to the Spirit that makes it all happen. The celebrated neurologist and author Oliver Sacks once said, "In forty years of medical practice, I have found only two types of non-pharmaceutical 'therapy' to be vitally important for patients with chronic neurological diseases: music and gardens."

FLIP THE SWITCH, UNPLUG, HIDE THE REMOTE

In making your home a sanctuary, try to establish rules with the other inhabitants—or with yourself if you live alone—to limit noise, technological stimulation, and other disturbances. Can you set a curfew so the house is quiet and tech-free the last hour or two before bed? Can you set standards for the morning so your days begin in peace? What about the first hour or so after arriving home from work? Perhaps these guideposts can include times for shared spiritual practice.

Speaking of noise, don't underestimate the jarring, nerve-jangling, peace-preventing impact of everyday clamor. I don't just mean egregious din like the roar of motorcycles and leaf blowers. I mean noise we adapt to and tune out but that registers on the nervous system like humidity registers on skin. The bedlam of blenders, hair dryers, freeway traffic, and, yes, television adds up, and it can be spiritually debilitating. My wife and I use headsets when we watch TV alone, to shield one another from the blare (I call the headset a Marriage Saver). Here's another tip: carry a pair of foam earplugs with you wherever you go. They come in handy, like a thermos or a fold-up umbrella.

Pay particular attention to digital disruption. At one point in his career, the jazz legend Miles Davis hired a future legend for his band: John Coltrane. The young saxophonist would launch into brilliant, ecstatic solos that ran far too long for the more disciplined Davis. Miles told him to show some restraint. Trane replied that he gets so absorbed in his improvisations that he loses all sense of time. Davis reportedly issued this command: "Just put down the horn, man."

Sometimes it's that simple.

Just put down the smartphone! Just shut off the TV! Just stop playing video games. Just switch from the news to a calming playlist.

Ah, but it's not always easy, is it? Like Coltrane, we get so wrapped up, we forget. Only we're not making glorious music; we're overwhelming our systems with more and more busyness and polluting our brains with aggravating news and cyberscreaming trolls.

Not that this is anything new. Back in the 19th century, when railroads started crisscrossing America and industrialization was speeding up the pace of life, Henry David Thoreau made this observation: "In proportion as our inward life fails, we go more constantly and desperately to the post-office. You may depend on it, that poor fellow who walks away with the greatest number of letters, proud of his extensive correspondence, has not heard from himself this long while."[23]

He could have said, "Just put down the mail, man."

Nowadays, a stroll to the village post office to pick up snail mail seems like an idyllic way to spend some time. It's what we might do if we rented a vacation cabin—only the cabin would be wired with Wi-Fi and streaming services, and we'd be texting as we walked back from the village. We might even have a headset on as we walked, listening to a podcast instead of birdsong.

I confess to being guilty of all the above. Thanks to technology, I've never been as well informed in my life. I record TV news programs to view when I'm doing routine tasks. I download podcasts for when I drive or walk to the store. Much of what I listen to is redundant or unnecessary. I tell myself, "Just put down the headset, man," but I don't always obey. So I write this to myself as well as to readers: to paraphrase the cartoon I cited in the preface, don't let the desire to be a well-informed citizen destroy your spiritual sanity. You could end up like the caged bird in another New Yorker cartoon, trembling, with crazed eyes all askew, and smoking a cigarette as one human says to another: "Maybe we shouldn't line her cage with the newspaper."

---

[23] From Thoreau's 1863 essay "Life without Principle."

Just put it down. Not always, of course. Not permanently. But more than you do now. In fact, don't even pick it up. Those times when you reflexively reach for your phone because there's a short break in the action? See if you can resist. It will feel weird. It will be uncomfortable. You'll think something bad will happen if you don't check your texts before the light turns green or the bank teller calls out "Next." In his helpful book *Fear Less*, Dean Sluyter calls that feeling "a wave of squirmy anxiety." Feel the squirm until it passes. By just saying no to device addiction, you will help prevent spiritual malaise.

You might even feel a sense of relief and a taste of peace. Take refuge in that, and consider how much stronger those feelings would be if you were to take a digital recess more often. How about checking your messages only once an hour, or once every three hours? How about unplugging for an entire day? Or something really radical, like a tech sabbatical? Cal Newport, author of *Digital Minimalism: Choosing a Focused Life in a Noisy World*, recommends abstaining from all input for a full month. Imagine that! But maybe you don't want to go that far. Can you at least replace what Newport calls "low-quality activities like mindless phone swiping and half-hearted binge-watching" with more rewarding offline activities? For example, the items in the Spiritual

Inventory you started in Chapter 4 or respites in the sacred spaces we discussed in this chapter.

 Maybe you'll discover, or *re*discover, sources of delight, or even the joy of doing absolutely nothing.

Before we move on to practices to apply in life's most disturbing moments, let's reiterate a key premise: wherever you are in time and space, and whatever the circumstances may be, you have within you the ultimate shelter. External sanctuaries are vital, but their primary function is to help us locate that ever-present internal temple. Then, as Thomas Merton put it, "Heaven is everywhere."

CHAPTER 8

When the Blitz Hits the Fan

Immediate Interventions

*Sit, be still, and listen, because you are drunk
and we are at the edge of the roof.*

— RUMI

My friend was driving alone on a four-lane boulevard in Los Angeles, minding her own business and listening to the news. Then she heard that immigrant children were being kept in cages at the Mexican border. She started screaming and swearing so much she nearly veered into the lane to her left. A driver in that lane thought she was shouting at him, so he yelled back. My friend, thinking the guy was arguing politics, turned to give him an earful, and . . . you guessed it, she rear-ended the car in front of her, which had stopped for a red light.

Just another day in the age of passionate overwhelm.

Sometimes, no matter how faithful we are to our regular spiritual practices, and no matter how resourceful we are in supplementing them, we get attacked by life and, in a flash, we're so infuriated, terrified, or otherwise deranged that we teeter on the brink of losing it. At such moments, it's easy to forget that peace is always a breath away. The grit and grime life throws at us blocks the door to our inner sanctuary; sometimes it even makes us forget it exists. The entrance is ever-present, though; we just need to find an opening. And there is always an opening. That's what Leonard Cohen meant when he sang that everything has a crack in it, which is how the light gets in.[24]

In moments of distress, the crack may be narrow; the illumination may flicker and last only an instant. But even that can be a great relief. If you're stumbling in a dark and unfamiliar room, even a momentary flash of light will help you get your bearings and relieve your anxiety.

If you need assurance that the divine light is ever-present, even in the darkest of circumstances, here's what Viktor Frankl observed in the Nazi death camp at Auschwitz: "In spite of all the enforced

---

[24] From the song "Anthem" (1992). The lyric is "There is a crack in everything / That's how the light gets in."

physical and mental primitiveness . . . it was possible for spiritual life to deepen." Some of the inmates, he said, "were able to retreat from their terribly surrounding ines in a life of inner riches and spiritual freedom." Frankl himself found some light while doing forced labor in a trench: "In a last violent protest against the hopelessness of imminent death, I sensed my spirit piercing through the enveloping gloom. I felt it transcend that hopeless, meaningless world, and from somewhere I heard a victorious 'Yes' in answer to my question of the existence of an ultimate purpose."[25]

No one reading this is in anything approaching the horrors of a concentration camp, but we all need access to our "inner riches" in troubling times, and we need spiritual safety valves when crises erupt. Here are some practices you might use in addition to those we've discussed in earlier chapters:

WATCH IT, FEEL IT, LET IT PASS

Sometime in the early 1970s, I was in an auditorium with about a thousand others listening to a talk by Maharishi Mahesh Yogi. Suddenly, a man rose from his aisle seat and started haranguing the famous guru for not using his platform to condemn the Vietnam War. A security guard moved toward

---

[25] From Viktor Frankl's book *Man's Search for Meaning*.

him, and some audience members formed a blockade in front of the stage. Everyone else watched to see what Maharishi would do. Seated cross-legged on a platform surrounded by flowers, he closed his eyes and sat there, rooted like a banyan tree, as the verbal assault continued. After what seemed like an hour but was actually a couple of minutes, the protestor quieted down. Maybe he ran out of things to say or was flustered by his target's nonreaction, but I suspect he was soothed by the calmness in the room. He was politely escorted out. A minute or so later, Maharishi opened his eyes, sniffed a long-stemmed rose, and said, "When the storm comes, it's best to be still and wait till it passes."

I took that as valuable advice and understood it to apply to internal storms as well as external ones. Have I succeeded in following the advice? LOL! But when I *have* emulated the less-is-more model, the rewards have been significant.

When emergency strikes, we may not have that luxury, of course; we have to spring into action. But in nonurgent situations, a pause can be the most effective move. In a raging hurricane of thought and emotion, you can feel severed from your Source. The ego takes control, and all it cares about is survival. That's when you say things you soon regret and take actions that are hard to repair. But the storms always pass. If we are protected by the spiritual equivalents of storm windows and emergency generators, our souls can remain safely hunkered down even as our minds are tossed around in the winds. But we have to remember to hold tight and wait it out.

The strategy turns out to have science behind it. "The healthiest way I know how to move through an emotion effectively is to surrender completely to that emotion when its loop of physiology comes over me," writes Jill Bolte Taylor, the neuroscientist mentioned in Chapter 5. "I simply resign to the loop and let it run its course for 90 seconds." That minute and a half is the average running time for the biochemical reaction. "This means that for 90 seconds you can watch the process happening, you can feel it happening, and then you can watch it go away," Dr. Taylor notes, adding that "any remaining emotional response is just the person choosing to stay in that emotional loop."

When the tornado hits, don't just do something—stand there. Actually, *sit* there if you can. Your instinct will be to do something—*anything*. But that fight-or-flight reaction is exactly what needs to be countered. I remember the sage advice I got from a farmer during my first winter in the New England countryside: "When that northern wind hits you in the face," he said, "you'll want to tighten up and lean into it. Don't. Just stand straight, relax your shoulders, and walk easy with it. If you resist, you'll get beat every time." Ever get a deep tissue massage? When it starts to hurt, you instinctively tighten up to resist the pressure. What's the advice? Relax into it.

So sit or stand. Close your eyes if you can; soft-focus if you can't. Shift your attention to your body. You will naturally be drawn to the strongest sensations. Just feel what's going on without analyzing, judging, or conceptualizing. If you feel pain, be with the pain. If you feel anguish, be with the anguish. If you feel rage, be with the rage. No pondering, no planning, no deciding, no sorting out cause and effect. Simply feel the sensations. Anticipate nothing, resist nothing.

You will invariably find—probably within that 90-second window—that the intensity diminishes. If feelings were solids, they'd become more like liquids, and eventually like gas or mist. Now you can reconnect to the wiser, more stable part of yourself. To use an Eastern metaphor, it's as if you've been riding underneath a galloping horse, holding on to its belly for dear life. Then the horse settles into an easy canter. Now you can clamber on top and grab the reins.

TAKE A BREATHER

In the midst of turmoil, the first suggestion you're likely to hear, whether from a spiritual leader, a doctor, or your Aunt Martha, is "Take a deep breath." It's a cliché, but it has the advantage of being sage advice. Deep breaths are quick, easy, convenient, inconspicuous, free, and effective. Yogis have always known this, and now scientists do too: when the stress response is triggered, the breath becomes shallow and rapid, whereas when we're at peace, the breath is slower and deeper. Hence, deep breaths reverse the emergency response. Spiritually speaking, breath is a gateway to the inner sanctuary; the Divine is, as Kabir put it, "the breath within the breath."

So take a few of them—take three, or five, or ten. Here are some tips for making deep breaths deeper and their impact stronger and more immediate.

Breathe with the Abdomen

Especially when under stress, we tend to breathe in by expanding our chests. This prevents the lungs from filling completely and leaves stale air unexpelled. To oxygenate fully, straighten up, relax your shoulders, and breathe in as you push out your abdomen—what yogis call belly breathing. This moves the diaphragm downward, drawing air into the lower portion of the lungs. As it happens, the area we call the abdomen is what the Japanese call *hara* and the Chinese *dantian*, the center of vital energy that plays a major role in traditional spiritual and martial arts practices. You might try adding a dimension to the inhale by imagining the air going all the way to the abdomen.

As your in-breath continues, you will find that your chest naturally expands, allowing the upper portion of the lungs to fill. On the out-breath, empty the upper lungs first, and pull in the abdomen to expel more air than you might be accustomed to. (Note that many physicians and stress-management experts advise adopting abdominal breathing as the norm, not just when countering the stress response.)

Hold It

As an option, retain the breath for varying lengths of time after the in-breath—or after both the in- and out-breaths. Notice the stillness that comes between breaths. Start with a two- or three-second hold and increase gradually. Don't overdo it; this is not a contest, and you're not a kid who needs to see how long it takes for your face to turn blue.

Nose and Mouth

Try breathing in through the nose and out through the mouth, exhaling with varying degrees of force. For example, expel the air while quietly voicing an open-mouthed *Haaaah*. Or purse your lips in a small circle and blow out a steady stream: *Hoooooo*. Do the same thing faster and more forcefully. And try a series of short exhales in the same manner. Generally speaking, the more agitated you feel, the more you'll want to purge the system with forceful exhales.

Elongate the Exhale

As we saw in Chapter 3, long exhales stimulate the vagus nerve, which in turn signals the parasympathetic system to reverse the fight-flight response. (One study found that subjects who extended their exhale were not only calmer but performed better on decision-making tests.) A traditional breathing instruction is to inhale for a count of four and exhale for a count of six. When you feel comfortable with that, try four and eight. Eventually, elongate the out-breath for as long as you can. Pull in your abdomen as you eject every cubic centimeter of air, as if trying to blow up a balloon to maximum size.

Then add this final touch: after you expel all the air, hold off the inhale until the body's survival instinct takes over and you breathe in automatically.

FOCUS ON THE SENSES

Another way to slow down a runaway mind is to fix one of your senses on a single object. This is more than a diversionary tactic; it's a way of shifting attention to the "present moment" that spiritual teachers urge us to enter.

Look

Wherever you are and whatever you're doing when the tornado strikes, there is always something to gaze at. Choose an object in your immediate environment. If it's pleasing to the eye or in some way interesting, that's fine but not necessary. Your own hand will do, or something from your pocket, or a picture on the wall, or the jacket on the person in front of you. You're not trying to extract some metaphysical meaning from the object, or to see God in it, or to do anything intentional at all. Just look at it. Gaze with innocent fascination, as if through the eyes of an infant or a curious Martian. That's all. If you find yourself drifting into a parade of thoughts—including wondering if you're doing this right—gently shift your sight to a different object or take a different angle on the first. Just gaze.

As we move on to the other four senses, let's note that vision is our most dominant sense. So closing your eyes makes it easier to focus on sound, smell, taste, and touch.

Listen

Pay attention to whatever sounds can be heard. Life usually offers up a lot more auditory stimulation than we realize, because the brain filters out extraneous sounds. Just hear what you hear. Don't interpret the sounds or try to figure out where they're coming from. As an alternative, listen closely to music, preferably without lyrics to ponder.

Smell

You may have noticed that the sense of smell is closely linked to memory and emotion. I couldn't possibly describe it, but I can effortlessly bring to mind the scent of my grandmother's home, 50 years after I last set foot in it. To short-circuit an emergency reaction, fixing your attention on any odor can work, but pleasant is obviously better than noxious because it makes it easy to linger. Since the olfactory environment is unpredictable, if you're scent-oriented you might want to carry a small vial of fragrant essential oil, such as lavender or rose, to break out in case of alarm.

Taste

Put something edible in your mouth. It might be a food you've eaten a thousand times, but savor it this time. Let it rest on top of your tongue. Swirl it from cheek to cheek. When you're ready to chew, do so slowly, without munching or chomping. Linger with each infusion of flavor. Swallow easily; don't gulp. Allow small morsels to slither slowly down your gullet and into your belly. (If food is not available, take the same approach with a beverage.)

Touch

I saved touch for last because it is the most immediately grounding of the senses. Touching an object absorbs the attention, and nothing could be more convenient or inconspicuous. Place your hand firmly on a table or the arm of a chair; grip your briefcase or purse; hold whatever is in your pocket; clasp your hands. You can do some of those things while walking too. You can also feel the weight of your backpack or your garments brushing against your skin. If you're driving, you can feel your grip on the steering wheel or the air from the window or vent. When you come to a stop, hold a water bottle, a key, a pen, the door handle, or anything else within reach. Whatever you touch, put your attention on the sensation. Again, don't analyze what you're touching; just feel it. Whenever you change the point of contact, notice the subtle shift in feeling: now heavy, now light; now smooth, now coarse. (Note: you might also combine touch intervention with deep breathing.)

Consider adding a sacred dimension to this strategy by keeping an especially meaningful object with you at all times. This is one reason Catholics carry rosaries and Hindus wear or carry *mala* beads. In fact, devotees of all traditions often carry a talisman in a pocket or purse, or pin one to their clothing, or attach an amulet to a necklace or bracelet. It could be a small picture of a revered person, a religious figurine, or a keepsake that brings to mind serenity, whether a gift from a loved one or a colorful stone you brought home from a beach vacation.

GET ABSORBED

You know the feeling artists and athletes describe as "being in the zone"? When you're so deeply involved in what you're doing that all sense of time dissolves and there's no space in your mind for troubles, regrets, and ruminations? When you're plugged into a larger energy flow, and your actions are unwilled and friction-free? When you might forget what's being done and the doer who's doing it? When you give no thought to performing well or looking good? Finding that zone is akin to grace.

What can you do that might be so utterly absorbing that you relinquish all concerns? Run? Knit? Dance around the room? Solve a puzzle? Read a story? Go bird-watching? Make love? Play a musical instrument? Take some swings in a batting cage? I thought of the last two examples when someone on Facebook posted two quotes from disparate sources: the jazz master Sonny Rollins—"You can't think and play at the same time"—and Yogi Berra—"How can you think and hit at the same time?"

If nothing comes immediately to mind, reflect on your past, and see if you can recall any such "in the flow" activities. Here are some spiritually absorbing options:

Spend Time with Children

If you have kids of your own, you already do this regularly, of course. But that might involve parenting pressure, so consider spending time with them in different ways. Take them to a place they've never been, or visit people they haven't met, and enjoy watching them respond to new situations. If you are not with children on a regular basis, go to a playground and watch them play. Volunteer at a day care center or a children's hospital. Their joy, their wonder, their innocence can remind you of what's important. If you're hurting, kids can heal you. If your heart has hardened, they'll soften it. And if they move you to contemplate the suffering of children caught up in natural disasters and human atrocities, or the precarious future they'll inherit thanks to our foolishness, go ahead and weep. That too is a form of grace, and it might lead you to ask how you can make things better for them.

Hang Out with Animals

I've met pet owners who say that frolicking with their dogs or cats is as devotional as prayer. Don't want pets? Maybe your neighbors have a dog or cat you can play with. Maybe there's an animal shelter nearby, or a stable, a dog park, or a veterinarian who can use a volunteer.

Help Someone

Ram Dass often told the story of asking his guru, Neem Karoli Baba, how to get enlightened. The answer? "Feed people." Nothing reduces an ego to the size of a mustard seed faster than caring for someone in need. Nothing is better at exposing the vanity of our worries. It doesn't matter if the beneficiary is a loved one or a stranger, as long as your heart leads the way.[26] (More on service in the next chapter.)

LET IT ALL OUT

Sometimes you just have to unload. The steam needs to be vented; the toxic sludge needs to be discharged; the demons need to be exorcised. If you're fortunate enough to have someone to whom you can express your feelings safely and constructively—a therapist, a compassionate friend, a family member—by all means do so. But you might need to vent in more visceral ways as well.

If breathing exercises, Yoga asanas, or a brisk workout can't give you sufficient physical release, go ahead and—safely and privately—explode. Pound a pillow, cushion, or mattress with your fists or a plastic

---

[26]   For an expert account of the transformative value of caregiving, read *The Soul of Care*, Dr. Arthur Kleinman's memoir of caring for a wife with Alzheimer's. Or listen to my interview of him on the *Spirit Matters* podcast.

Wiffle ball bat. Smash. Bash. Pummel. Beat that thing to an imaginary pulp.

You might want to amplify the muscular catharsis with screams and shouts (assuming no one will hear you and call the police). Don't hold anything back. Shriek. Roar. Holler. Curse. Give yourself permission to throw a tantrum.

Does that sound *unspiritual*? Well, ask yourself this: How spiritual is it to suppress your feelings and let them eat away at your soul like acid? How spiritual would it be if the suppressed feelings were to leak out in the form of obnoxious behavior? Think of it as Holy Rage. You'll be in the good company of biblical prophets and other historical figures who raged about injustice and human suffering. You can make it explicitly spiritual by directing your fury at God if you're theistically inclined, or at the gods if you're pantheistic, or at the vast indifference of the universe if you favor an impersonal cosmology.

No need to feel foolish. There is nothing rational about this; it's not about making sense. No need to feel guilty either. Scolding the Almighty doesn't make you a heretic or an ungrateful wretch. Rebuking the Divine is a time-honored tradition. Think of it as a form of prayer. If you need a familiar role model, revisit the book of Job. The protagonist, Job, is usually presented as an exemplar of faith, but in the story he refuses to let the Almighty off the hook for what he considers injustice. And what happens in the end? He is richly rewarded and beloved by his Lord.

Or contemplate this story: A man in India roams through his village every day cursing God at the top of his lungs. The villagers fear that the whole community will be cursed, but they can't get him to stop. One day the man climbs to the roof of a temple and announces that he's going to die. He sits down, closes his eyes, and calmly passes on. At that very moment, a magnificent chorus rings out in song. No one knows where the celestial music is coming from. They ask the wisest woman in the village. She says the angels are welcoming the dying man to their heavenly abode.

The people are incredulous. "But he profaned the name of God! He cursed the Lord!"

"If you remember God one one-hundredth of the time he did," says the wise woman, "you too will be liberated."

But maybe pounding and screaming are not your style. Perhaps instead—or in addition—you would rather vent the *write* way. Writing adds an element of cognitive processing to the emotional release, and there is strong evidence that written expression is healing on many levels. James Pennebaker, a psychologist at the University of Texas, did a series of

experiments in which one group wrote about emotionally significant experiences and another wrote
about ordinary things. After doing this exercise for 20
minutes on three consecutive days, the subjects in the
first group showed marked improvement in various
measures of well-being, including reduced depression
and anxiety and, months later, improved blood pressure, immune function, relationships, memory, and
work success.[27] Based on her own research, Harvard
psychologist Susan David described people who ben-
efited from writing exercises in an almost yogic way:
"In the process of writing, they were able to create
the distance between the thinker and the thought,
the feeler and the feeling, that allowed them to gain a
new perspective, unhook, and move forward."[28]

Whether you write longhand in a notebook or
type into a digital platform, pouring out your feelings produces physical and psychological benefits,
according to studies on the practice of journaling.
You might also air out your thoughts in letter form.
Note that *you will never send this letter.* It will be read
by no one but you. You can delete it, tear it up, or
burn it when you're done. So write with a recipient
in mind. It could be a public figure, a friend or family
member, a mentor or role model, a revered spiritual

---

[27] For more information, see Dr. Pennebaker's book *Writing to Heal: A Guided Journal for Recovering from Trauma and Emotional Upheaval* (New Harbinger, 2004).

[28] From Susan David's book *Emotional Agility: Get Unstuck, Embrace Change, and Thrive in Work and Life.*

figure. The imagined recipient can be living or dead (e.g., an ancestor). It could be God in whatever form suits your beliefs.

The key is to write without censoring yourself. Set aside ample time, and hold nothing back. Pay no mind to grammar, spelling, syntax, or punctuation. Don't worry about style, structure, or consistency. It doesn't have to be logical or even coherent. What matters is your emotional truth, not factual truth. This is not a news broadcast or a social media post; it's a way to purge your system of outrage, pain, fury, dread, sorrow, indignation, or anything else you're feeling. Probe deeply into your heart and mind, and don't stop writing until you feel complete, even if you end up repeating yourself many times.

If the written word is not your thing, or if your fingers get numb from writing so much, you can do your venting orally. Find a place where no one will hear you, and let loose out loud. Turn on a recorder if you think you'll want to hear the tirade another time, or express yourself to someone you imagine is sitting opposite you.

SMILE

"Sometimes your joy is the source of your smile," Thich Nhat Hanh teaches, "but sometimes your smile can be the source of your joy." That statement is corroborated by a scientific concept called the facial feedback hypothesis. In a nutshell, experiments show that changing our expressions can change our emotions, presumably through some neural interaction between facial muscles and the brain. For example, subjects who are instructed to smile during a social gathering report that they enjoy the event more than those who are *not* told to smile. Maybe Mona Lisa was on to something.

Try it. While you're reading this, smile. It doesn't matter how you actually feel; just widen your lips in the shape of a smile, as if someone was about to take your picture. Emulate the statues of Buddha—not the jolly laughing ones, the ones with the half smile of unshakable contentment.

See? Something happens, doesn't it? Try it when you're in a rotten mood. You might be surprised by the subtle shift in your emotional state. One caveat: don't go overboard and walk around with a perpetual grin like you're auditioning for the role of the Joker. Whatever grace you gain from the facial feedback loop you'll lose when no one wants to hang out with you.

LAUGH

Life on Earth comes with a kind of planetary subscription to a vast number of channels. Much of the fare is tragedy, of course, and there's plenty of serious drama, action-adventure, horror, romance, and high-stakes suspense thrillers. But there's also a lot of dark comedy, satire, parody, goofball slapstick, and sitcoms with wacky characters doing dumb things. Switching to the humor channels can be a blessed form of relief when all around you are trage-dies and unhappy endings. All it requires is a shift of attention, because it's really nutty out there.

Finding something to laugh at does not require betraying your moral principles or watering down your concerns about the world. You're just getting some karmic relief through comic relief. Is it spiri-tual? Why not? The cheeriest chucklers I've ever met are profoundly spiritual people, including clerics and gurus. They recognize that the human condi-tion is serious drama, but also a farce. They'd proba-bly agree with the French philosopher Voltaire, who thought of God as a comedian whose audience is afraid to laugh.

It goes without saying that laughter is not always appropriate. But it's also true that we suffer when we take our lives too seriously. Sometimes, humor is the best healer, as any nurse can tell you. Sometimes, making someone chuckle in the midst of difficulties can be as compassionate as a hug. "He deserves paradise who makes his companions laugh," it says in the Koran. Perhaps that's why some of the greatest American humorists were Jews and African Americans, in whose communities laughter was an antidote for pain. In *Fiddler on the Roof*, when the Jews are yet again forced into exile without warning, the main character, Tevye, says, "Maybe that's why we always wear our hats."

Reasons to laugh are not hard to find if you're open to them. Hang out with witty people—not the frivolous ones but those who can giggle at life's absurdities as much as they weep for the catastrophes. Take a break from the news and watch a funny movie. Or mix news and laughs by tuning in to late-night talk shows. I record them to watch with my breakfast, and frankly I don't know how I would have made it through the past few years without them and NPR's newsy game show *Wait Wait . . . Don't Tell Me!* They remind me that theologian Reinhold Niebuhr was right when he said, "Humor is a prelude to faith and laughter the beginning of prayer."[29]

---

[29]   From Niebuhr's book *Discerning the Signs of the Times: Sermons for Today and Tomorrow.*

LEARN

The spiritual perspective that makes the most sense to me says we are born on this planet to learn and grow. Everything that happens—the good and the bad, the beautiful and the ugly—is part of the curriculum. And the most difficult courses can be the best vehicles for evolutionary change.

Extracting useful lessons from heartbreak and calamity requires a certain amount of acceptance. Not approval. Not acquiescence. Not complacency or indifference. What I mean by acceptance is *not wishing things were different.* Because that wish—that desire for reality not to be real, but to turn miraculously into something else—is not only a waste of energy but the very root of unnecessary suffering. When you accept what is and declare your intent to learn from it, transformation becomes possible. You may not be able to change your external circumstances, but you can certainly renovate *yourself* if you learn the right lessons. Approaching the situation as homework for a required course can take some of the sting out of painful conditions and help ensure that next time you will respond from a more evolved position.

It's all grist for the mill. Our task is to convert what appear to be obstacles on the path into the path itself. Ask yourself how you can make a spiritual practice out of what is presented to you in this moment, in this place. What is the study guide for this assignment? Something about patience, perhaps? Something about how you interpret life's ups and downs? About your expectations? About non-attachment? About fear? Anger? Love? Compassion? Is it that you haven't given enough? Or that you've tried to give *too* much? Are you being urged to identify and heal old wounds? Are you being called to a new type of action or a new way of being?

Seeing whatever occurs as part of your lesson plan is another gateway to the inner sanctuary. It makes even the hard stuff a gift. Welcome whatever rings your doorbell as you would a guest, Rumi advises in his poem "The Guest House." Here are the last two stanzas:

> *The dark thought, the shame, the malice,*
> *meet them at the door laughing,*
> *and invite them in.*
>
> *Be grateful for whoever comes,*
> *because each has been sent*
> *as a guide from beyond.*

If you can attain that level of acceptance in the midst of catastrophe and torment, you are blessed. Consider expressing your gratitude to whatever force, power, person, or deity you believe is responsible.

WE NOW PAUSE FOR A REALITY CHECK

If you try to apply the suggestions in this chapter and find that the calmness they produce is short-lived, or that you recover nicely from an initial earthquake only to get rocked by aftershocks, don't be discouraged. Such experiences are to be expected. Methods are not magic. Practices are not pills. Equanimity in the midst of turbulence can't be coerced, forced, or willed into existence; it can only be encouraged and intended. We can't always be as inwardly still as a flame in a windless place, to use another yogic metaphor. But we can move in that direction. The capacity develops over time, usually in fits and starts, as the inner flame flickers and dies and has to be relit.

If we diligently apply tools like the ones in this book, we can speed our progress toward the ideal. But along the way, we have to manage our expectations. The rewards of practice don't accrue in a linear, predictable fashion like compound interest, and the path is more like a bumpy road with erratic traffic signals than an interstate highway.

So don't expect miracles. And don't think you're a failure if you get sucked into the whirlwind yet again, or if you get overwhelmed by the same kind of events you were able to endure with dignity and poise just the day before. You are not spiritually inadequate. You did nothing wrong. This is a time to practice the Reverse Golden Rule: Do unto yourself as you would have yourself do unto others. Give yourself the kindness and compassion you'd give your neighbor. You're an imperfect human like the rest of us, so lighten up. Make radical self-acceptance a spiritual practice of its own.

See if you can turn your discontent into fuel for the next phase of the journey. When a new storm surge comes, instead of becoming upset with yourself for getting all shook up, face the anguish and frustration head-on. Feel the feelings without resistance. Only this time, try—without strain, without manipulation, without actually *trying*—to witness the feelings from a position of some mental distance. To the extent you can, fall back to the vantage point of your undisturbed Self and watch the blizzard of feelings and thoughts as if from a window in a safe, warm home. Even a little of that witnessing can help you turn thoughts like *I'm angry* and *I'm scared* into *Anger/fear is being felt at this moment*. That may seem like a minor difference, but think about it: one is an "I am" statement—almost an identity stamp— while the other suggests a temporary situation that touches your mind and body but not your deepest Self. Which is exactly what it is.

If that sense of separation from your thoughts and actions does not come naturally, I repeat: you're not a failure, you're not spiritually deficient, you're not screwing up, and you did not miss out on some special trick in the previous pages. Think of it this way: just having that vision of spiritual progress is a sign of progress. So keep on truckin' along your path with your inventory of practices at hand. And try to remember, as the next and last chapter suggests, that it's not all about *you*.

CHAPTER 9

Sacred Citizenship

Giving Back from the Inside Out

Do not be daunted by the insurmountability of the world's grief. Do justly now. Love mercy now. Walk humbly now. You are not obligated to complete the work, but neither are you free to abandon it.

— THE TALMUD

A little more than a century ago, Evelyn Underhill, the author of the seminal text *Mysticism* (1911), produced a slim volume titled *Practical Mysticism*. She called it "a little book for normal people." When the First World War broke out, she considered canceling publication. Then she realized that the book's message was not only relevant in those dire circumstances; it was necessary. Transcendent spiritual experience, she argued, "does not wrap its initiates in a selfish and otherworldly calm, isolate

them from the pain and effort of the common life."
On the contrary, because those experiences "reveal
to us a world of higher truth and greater reality," she
said, their impact is even stronger "when confronted
by the overwhelming disharmonies and sufferings
of the present time."

What was true amid the crisis of 1915 is just as
true today. Our "disharmonies and sufferings" are
different, of course, and in many ways more complex
and enigmatic. But underlying our myriad troubles
is a fundamental spiritual crisis—a collective bank-
ruptcy of the soul that demands a spiritual response.

To paraphrase Michelle Obama, when the world
goes low, we have to go high—in fact, to the Highest. We are called not only to wake up spiritually but
also to wise up and show up. Just as hate can only be
countered by love, darkness can only be eliminated
by light, and every candle counts. Once our individual flames are lit from within, it is imperative that
we shine them somewhere, however dim or incon-
sistent they may be.

It must be said that some spiritual teachings
do foster what Underhill called "a selfish and otherworldly calm" and *do* counsel isolation from "the
pain and effort of the common life." Otherworldly
escapism can be found in sectors of every faith, and
also among independent seekers who either have

good reason to pull away from the fray or are misinformed about certain spiritual tenets. Take, for
example, nonattachment. This central teaching in
both Eastern and Western traditions has been taken
to mean indifference and has led to withdrawal
from worldly responsibilities. It emphatically does
not imply either of those. In the Bhagavad Gita, for
example, the advice on nonattachment is given to a
warrior on the battlefield, and no one would want a
soldier fighting in a righteous cause to not care how
things turn out.

Similarly, the theory of karma is *not* a rationale for shrugging off suffering and injustice, as
in remarks such as "I feel bad for those people, but
they're reaping what they sowed, and they have to
pay their debt." If the laws of karma are true, that
would surely be the case. However, this would also
be true: *we* will pay the price for what we do or don't
do in response to suffering and oppression. Karmic
law may not be kind to those who use profound spiritual concepts as an excuse for complacency.

The same is true of phrases like "It's God's will"
and "Thy will be done." Everything may be in God's
hands, as is often said, but what if God wants our
hands to pitch in? What if God's will works through
our will? As for the expression "Let go and let God,"
Islam has an incisive saying: "Trust in Allah, but tie

your camel to the post." We all bear some responsibility for the condition of the world, and we are called upon to act in the spirit of Judaism's *tikkun olam*—to improve, or repair, the world.

BE THE CHANGE

Be a blazing fire of truth, be a beauteous blossom of love, and be a soothing balm of peace.

— Sufi saying

There is no evidence that Mahatma Gandhi actually said "Be the change you wish to see in the world," as bumper stickers and social media posts claim, but whoever did say it was onto something: a society can't live up to its highest ideals if the individuals who constitute the society don't, just as a forest can't be green if the trees are not. That's why the airline announcement to secure your own oxygen mask before helping others with theirs has become a useful metaphor for helpers and social activists: you can do more for others if you first take care of yourself. As Swami Satchidananda put it: "Find the peace in yourself so that you can help others realize their own peace. . . . A razor must be sharpened before it is useful."

This is not some call to sacrificial martyrdom. By infusing your actions with laudable qualities that tend to develop with spiritual practice— love, generosity, kindness, etc.—you improve your social environment and, therefore, your own happiness and growth, along with everyone else's.

The Shadow Knows

Paramahansa Yogananda suggested this practice to his followers: every night, before going to sleep, introspect deeply about your behavior that day. Honestly assess your flaws and shortcomings, and write down how you will replace them with positive traits.

Like all spiritual teachers, Yogananda urged us to identify with the infinite Self, not the personality we think we are—and, *at the very same time,* improve that personality and align it more closely with divine goodness. As his guru did with him, he admonished disciples to "learn to behave!"

Our true nature is infinite . . . but we are also finite beings. Our Essence is flawless . . . and we are also flawed individuals. We need to transcend our small selves . . . and also be better small selves. So we have to ask ourselves: Am I doing anything that makes the world a little worse? A bit meaner? A tad more tense? Am I polluting the atmosphere with senseless anger, jealousy, resentment, selfishness, or hostility? Can I instead summon up more compassion? More love? More empathy?

On the spiritual path, we often resist peering into the darker corners of our psyches. We would rather turn toward the light and focus on the higher truths. But, as Carl Jung said, "There is no light without shadow and no psychic wholeness without imperfection." We all have deficiencies, neuroses, and negative tendencies. Working to diminish those shadowy elements helps us spiritually by reducing the struggle, disharmony, and tension in our environment. It also helps repair one small corner of the world.

Many seekers fall prey to thinking that if we just meditate longer, or pray harder, or chant more often—or you name it—all our psychological gook will wash away like dirt down a drain. Instead, they usually find that their baggage clings, and tendencies they thought they were done with reappear at inconvenient moments, like when they disagree with a spouse, or lose a job, or visit their parents. The belief (more of a hope really) that spiritual methods alone will resolve all our issues is a trap. Therapists call it "spiritual bypassing," a form of avoidance that has been a roadblock on many a spiritual path. We owe it to ourselves and those we care about to strengthen our weakest links while at the same time remembering our inherent worth as offspring of the Divine.

Be More Perfect

A Zen master was scolding disciples for misbehaving. One bold student challenged him: "But Master, you said the universe is perfect as is, and so are we."

"Yes, you are perfect," the master replied. "Be more perfect."

How can you be a more perfect partner, parent, son/daughter, neighbor, co-worker, friend, citizen?

One ethical precept universally extolled is what we call the Golden Rule. "Do unto others what you would have them do unto you" comes from Jesus in the Sermon on the Mount (Matthew 7:12). In the same part of the world, in the same era—most likely before Jesus was born—the famed rabbi Hillel stated it another way. When he was challenged by a student to teach him the Torah in the brief time that he, the student, could stand on one foot, Hillel replied, "What is hateful to you, do not do to others." The rest of the Torah, he added, was only commentary. Followers of Islam know it this way: "No one of you is a believer until he desires for his brother that which he desires for himself." In ancient China, the rule was attributed to Confucius: "What you do not want done to yourself, do not do to others." Hindus will find it in the epic Mahabharata as "Do nothing to others which, if done to you, would cause you pain," and Buddhists know it as "Hurt not others with that which pains yourself."

The rule may seem like a cliché, but it is golden because, in order to put it into practice, we have to marshal a host of other virtues, such as compassion, empathy, forgiveness, generosity, humility, integrity, kindness, love, patience, reverence . . . and I'm sure you can think of others.

Cultivating morally upright attributes deepens our alignment with the Divine and adds a measure of sanity to this crazy world. One good practice is to focus on a single desired quality at a time, perhaps for a week. During that period, look for ways to exercise that muscle. Be vigilant about recognizing your own resistance, and honestly assess why you're doing it.

Another approach is to use the kind of guided visualizations athletes and others employ to improve performance. Choose an attribute you wish to develop. Set aside 5 or 10 minutes; close your eyes; settle into a calm state of mind; and imagine yourself exhibiting the trait in different situations—at home, at work, when socializing, and so forth. What would it feel like? How would you speak? What would you look like to others? How would you respond in diffi-cult situations?

Using the power of imagination in this way instructs your subconscious to substitute desirable behavior for the unhelpful patterns of the past. Work on areas you most want to improve, and repeat the exercise as often as needed.

Cultivating a Cardinal Virtue

Compassion is central to the spiritual enter-prise because it's both the natural expression of a heart touched by the Divine and a pathway *to* the Divine. Buddhists consider it so vital that they devel-oped techniques to unfold, enlarge, and strengthen our capacity for compassion. The following pair of mental practices are widely used by Buddhists and non-Buddhists alike.

Metta[30]

There are countless variations of this method, all of which follow the same basic pattern: feeling compassion first for ourselves and then for a series of others who are located further and further from the locus of our care.

---

[30] *Metta* is typically translated from the original Pali as "loving-kindness."

Sit in a quiet, comfortable place, as you would for any meditative practice. If you wish, do a breathing exercise and/or meditate before beginning. When you're ready, slowly and silently, without moving your lips, recite the following sentences. Pause slightly between recitations, and observe the feelings and sensations that arise.

> *May I be free from suffering.*
> *May I be healthy and strong.*
> *May I be peaceful and at ease.*
> *May I be happy.*

Rest in the awareness of that intention for a minute or two—or longer if you're so inclined.

Now shift the focus from yourself to someone whose well-being matters to you. You may want to visualize that person as you intone the phrases within:

> *May [name] be free from suffering.*
> *May [name] be healthy and strong.*
> *May [name] be peaceful and at ease.*
> *May [name] be happy.*

Rest for a period of time. Are the feelings and sensations that came up different from what you felt when you directed loving-kindness to yourself?

Now shift attention to someone for whom you have neutral feelings—a distant relative, an acquaintance, a neighbor, or a coworker, for instance. Repeat the process with that person's name. When you finish, rest and note how it felt compared to the previous segment.

Next, focus on someone for whom you have negative feelings. Someone who aggravates you. Someone you disapprove of. Someone you can't stand. You might feel resistance with this one. Do it with as much sincerity as you can muster. During the rest phase, reflect on what came up for you, and ponder what needs to happen in order for you to do the practice and really mean it.

In the final step, we shift from a specific person to the welfare of the planet. Begin each sentence with the phrase "May all beings . . ." You should have no trouble sincerely wishing peace, happiness, and freedom from suffering for all of humanity and all other sentient beings.

Tonglen

In Tibetan, the word *tonglen* means "giving and taking" (sometimes translated as "sending and receiving"). In this practice, when we breathe in, we imagine removing something negative from another person and taking it into ourselves. On the exhale, we give or send something beneficial to the same person.

Assume a comfortable position in a peaceful location, close your eyes, and settle into a calm but alert state. Choose someone who is suffering physically, mentally, economically, or otherwise. It could be someone you know very well or a person you just know about. Visualize her or him standing before you, enveloped by a thick, dark cloud. The cloud represents this person's pain.

As you breathe in deeply, imagine you are pulling that noxious cloud away from that person and drawing it into yourself. As the opaque smoke enters your chest, imagine it becoming lighter and lighter in color until it is a radiant gold. Know this to be the compassionate light of loving-kindness. See it surround your heart.

.Then, as you exhale, send that resplendent light to the suffering person. See it envelop him or her, alleviating every burden.

Continue in this manner for a comfortable period of time, breathing in the cloud of suffering and breathing out the warm glow of compassion.

Once you're accustomed to doing tonglen in a meditative way, try using it at other times. When you're out and about and see people who are in some way disturbed, visualize that dark cloud around them; breathe it in; convert it to light; and exhale radiant compassion. You can also do it for entire populations suffering from war, oppression, or natural disasters.

Don't be surprised if you start wondering if these practices really help other people. The question may be unanswerable, but this much is definitely true: doing tonglen and metta will help *you*. Your compassion muscles will be strengthened, and you will more fully appreciate this insight from the Christian mystic Thomas Merton: "The whole idea of compassion is based on a keen awareness of the interdependence of all these living beings, which are all part of one another, and all involved in one another."[31]

Namaste

The attributes we value most are rooted in our sense of kinship with other human beings. That sense of belonging makes it natural to offer love, kindness, and forgiveness beyond the circle of our immediate family. And the further out that circle of care ripples, the closer we get to the saints who know in their bones that we are, at the deepest level, separate from nothing and no one.

---

[31] Merton reportedly made the statement in what turned out to be his final speech, two hours before his accidental death in 1968.

No single word captures the spirit of that realization as well as the traditional Hindu greeting *namaste*. The word is now familiar in the West, but when I travel in India, it is always humbling and heartwarming to be greeted by it (or with the somewhat more reverential *namaskar*). The standard interpretation of *namaste*—"I honor the divinity within you"[32]—suggests that we are not just connected to one another; we *are* one another. Sure, the gesture can be routine, and its profound implication—that we should treat others as ourselves—is easily ignored. But many find that saying namaste, along with the traditional gesture of a slight bow with palms together prayerfully at the chest, shakes loose their empathy and compassion in ways that other greetings do not.

Joseph Deitch, in his book *Elevate,* suggests using the term not only outwardly but as an internal spiritual practice. Simply intone namaste mentally while looking at another person, who needn't have any inkling of what you're doing. First, sense the divinity within yourself. Then feel or imagine that same sacred Essence within the other person. And allow the two divine sparks to connect energetically and become One.

---

32   Alternatively, "I honor" can be translated as "I salute," "I recognize," or "I bow to."

This exercise has the obvious advantage of being entirely inconspicuous. You can do it when meeting someone, when making eye contact at a distance, or by silently directing your humble greeting to strangers on the street, in shops, in lobbies, on subways, and anywhere else. The practice can be transformative if you bring to it the intent and spirit baked into the meaning of *namaste*.

Cut Yourself a Break

What does the Lord require of you?
To act justly and to love mercy and
to walk humbly with your God.

— MICAH 6:8

Any attempt to upgrade your character is likely to make you acutely aware of the gap between where you are and where you want to be. It's a good idea to acknowledge that chasm and see if you're resisting change—and why. But while honest assessment is important, so is cutting yourself some slack. Anyone with a decent moral compass knows the right thing to do in most instances. But we all have egos, and we all have selfish desires. Those desires insert their priorities into our thoughts and our actions, and the ego tricks us into justifying behavior that doesn't serve us spiritually.

Be patient. The residue of the past—what yogis call *samskaras*—does not go away overnight. Unwanted patterns can persist, and they'll rise up when least expected to remind you that you're human and have a ways to go. It doesn't mean your efforts have been in vain. It means you've been handed another opportunity to learn. So don't be unkind to yourself for not being kind enough. Don't be too hard on yourself for being hard on others. Extend to yourself the compassion, patience, and forgiveness you wish to offer the rest of humanity.

Aiming for goodness is not some kind of religious insurance policy that pays off in the afterlife; it's a transformational pathway with benefits in the here and now. When you walk through life like a spiritual Johnny Appleseed, planting loving-kindness wherever you go, you align with the Eternal; you link your soul to other souls; and the karmic dividends will arrive in self-addressed envelopes at your doorstep.

And one more little miracle: spiritual virtues are sustainable, self-renewing resources; the more you use them, the more of them you have.

HERE'S LOOKING AT YOU, KID

I slept and dreamt that life was joy.
I woke and saw that life was service.
I acted and behold! service was joy.

— RABINDRANATH TAGORE

Recently, I had occasion to once again see the closing sequence of the 1942 movie classic *Casablanca*. In it, Rick (Humphrey Bogart) and Ilsa (Ingrid Bergman) are at an airstrip. A prop plane is ready for takeoff. Nazis are on their way to stop it. We viewers want the couple to live happily ever after. But this is wartime. Rick tells Ilsa to board the plane without him and escape with her freedom-fighter husband. "I'm no good at being noble," he says, "but it doesn't take much to see that the problems of three little people don't amount to a hill of beans in this crazy world."

Previously cynical, Rick has come to see that he must do his bit in the struggle against tyranny, no matter the cost. We get teary-eyed, but our spirits soar. We like to think that we too would sacrifice for a righteous cause. Well, it's not World War II, and we may not have to turn away from the love of our lives, but the world is in perilous shape, and we are all needed.

You don't have to be a moral giant like Gandhi, King, or Mandela to raise your hand and do what you can to make the crazy world a bit more sane. No gesture is too small. No action is too late. I meet people who are so discouraged by world conditions that they've lost all hope, and therefore all motivation. Others are unmotivated for a different reason: their lives are good, and so far they're unscathed by the troubles afflicting so many others. To the first group, I would say, instead of asking "What's the use?" ask "What can I do?" Every brick helps erect the edifice of Goodness. To the second group, I would paraphrase the contemporary spiritual teacher Mata Amritanandamayi ("the hugging saint"): if you're on a rooftop, safe from the fire on the ground floor, it's a good idea to help put out flames, because they'll get to you soon enough. To which I would add: stay tuned. You may not be driven to action now, but one day, as you move forward on your spiritual path, your moral sensibility just might get aroused, and you'll feel moved to take on the problems around you. It's the natural instinct of a heart filled to overflowing.

What will be your offering? Perhaps your circumstances or predilections dictate that you focus on your immediate environment, making your home, your street, your neighborhood a safer, friendlier, more harmonious place. You might have the time and inclination to focus only on your family—on raising your kids to be good citizens or banding together to reduce your carbon footprint by cutting back on meat, taking quicker showers, or refilling a thermos instead of buying plastic bottles of water. Perhaps you're moved to help a needy person close to home—a single mom who's overwhelmed, a disabled vet, an elderly neighbor with limited mobility—or to volunteer at a school, hospital, kennel, homeless shelter, or recycling campaign. Wherever you are, whatever your passions, if you look around, you'll surely find people, organizations, and causes that can use your help.

If you're motivated to expand your domain, perhaps there are regional, national, or global issues to which you can lend time and energy. Education? Health care? Food and nutrition? Poverty and homelessness? Climate change? Maybe one of those will activate your inner activist, and if you don't have time to offer, you can always write a check. If political action appeals to you, perhaps you'll consider throwing your hat into the ring and running for the school board, neighborhood council, legislature, or other public office. If that's too daunting, help a candidate you admire, and don't underestimate the merits of seemingly small gestures like canvassing from the comfort of your home or helping people register to vote. At a *satsang* (spiritual gathering) in India a few years ago, a swami was fielding questions from devotees. One woman asked what she could do about an onerous problem in their region. Everyone expected a profound esoteric insight or a "spiritual" appraisal of the situation. Instead, they got a crisp, one-word answer: "Vote."

How May I Help?

Don't assume that only sacrificial and arduous activities are worthy of being called service. On the contrary, it's usually best to find opportunities that suit your nature and align with your sensibilities, views, and natural gifts. Why would an energizing, jubilant act be any less meaningful than somber toil? You'll not only bring excellence to the task; you'll also transmit your joy to those you serve. There's a reason "Service with a Smile" is used as a corporate mantra. We're called upon to happily help, not to be martyrs. "Don't ask yourself what the world needs," advised Howard Thurman, the revered theologian and pastor who was a mentor to Martin Luther King Jr. "Ask yourself what makes you come alive, and then go do that, because what the world needs is people who have come alive."[33]

---

[33] From the Sounds True audio CD *The Living Wisdom of Howard Thurman: A Visionary for Our Time.*

At the same time, you'll derive more from service if you leave your ego at home. Make your activity an offering to the Supreme Good, however you conceive of it. Do it humbly, with no concern for recognition or reward. This is the recognized pathway of Karma Yoga, which asks us to serve selflessly, putting our full attention on performing the task at hand without attachment to the outcome. Such humble service loosens the bondage of ego. That's what makes it a powerful spiritual practice—if we avoid the trap of puffing ourselves up too much for being so selfless.

The healthiest and most beneficial service flows naturally from spiritual abundance, the way philanthropy spills from decent people with wealth. "What do I want?" shifts to "How can I help?" Doing for others becomes as natural as protecting a child. And as the arms of empathy open wider and wider, the Sanskrit maxim *vasudhaiva kutumbakam*—"the world is one family"—becomes a lived reality. And who doesn't want to help their family? At the same time, it's always a good idea to monitor ourselves to make sure our intentions and behavior are consistent with our spiritual values.

If you need added incentive, check out the studies that reveal what the wise have always known: selfless service serves the self. Data show that people who devote time to helping others tend to be happier and more content than those who are always looking out for number one. They report higher levels of satisfaction, optimism, and purpose. They're healthier too, physically and emotionally, and on the average live longer. If you want to be unhappy, I once heard a guru say, think about yourself all the time. If, instead, you think of the needs of others, even occasionally, you'll feel the freedom of transcending your ego. That's why Mother Teresa had terminally ill patients pray for one another instead of for themselves.

SPIRITUAL ACTIVISM

In my student years, I marched, organized, and protested, mainly against the Vietnam War but also on behalf of social justice issues. Back then I accepted the Marxist maxim that religion was the opium of the people. My actions were righteous, but my inner life was a mess. I found my way to the spiritual path and before long switched from political to spiritual activism. I saw that social change was an inside job, and I was convinced that world peace would come only when enough individuals found inner peace. So I joined in group meditations that I believed purified the environment like a natural disinfectant, and I trained to be a meditation teacher. I used to say I was bringing light to the darkness, one mantra at a time.

All these years later, that perspective still seems valid. It also seems naïve. The world did not change the way spiritual idealists like me expected it to. Inner transformation is clearly not enough, at least on the scale we've so far accomplished. But this too is obvious: activism *without* personal transformation is also not enough. The times call for a holistic, inside-out response to our collective crises. We need social activists who work on their inner lives, and we also need spiritually evolving people who care enough to make their presence felt.

When I say this, I'm often asked what a spiritual solution would look like. Which party or system would be most spiritual? Which political ideology or economic philosophy? Which policy on immigration, abortion, climate change, crime, education . . . you name it. I have opinions, but I can't say there are definitive answers. Maybe those are the wrong kinds of questions. In a complex, fast-changing world, policies need to change creatively with the facts and circumstances. Attachment to doctrines and ideologies can compound fanaticism and further divide one group from another. Rigid ideologues

are often so unmoved by evidence that they remind
me of football coaches who stubbornly stick to their
game plan no matter what happens on the field.

It would seem that a truly spiritual response to
vexing social issues would be flexible, creative, and
open minded. It would recognize that the success of
any program depends on the quality of the individuals who carry it out, just as great choreography needs
talented dancers and winning sports teams need
excellent players. "We can't solve problems by using
the same kind of thinking we used when we created
them," Einstein reputedly said. Nor can we untangle
a moral morass with the same hearts that produced
it. We need spiritually illumined, morally mature
citizens the way a garden needs healthy flowers.

I am not suggesting that anyone who steps onto
a spiritual path magically turns into a moral para-
gon and an intuitive genius. I've traveled in spiritual
circles for half a century, and I've witnessed a shock-
ing amount of dishonesty, selfishness, and con-
striction of the heart. But I've also seen more of the
opposite. And therein lies realistic hope. People on a
deep, transformational path are, in varying degrees,
tapping into the universal Source of energy, intelligence, and love. It seems reasonable to conclude,
therefore, that each individual's impact on society

would grow more positive with each step of progress they take along an authentic spiritual path.

To be specific, people blessed with a strong connection to the Divine are more likely to be guided by a strong moral compass; to be motivated by higher goals than greed or status; to view the human landscape with empathy and compassion; to know that the pursuit of happiness is not satisfied by fleeting pleasures or the acquisition of wealth; to appreciate that human destiny is linked to the natural environment; to recognize and value the shared humanity of all racial, religious, and ethnic groups; to balance emotional intelligence with discernment and respect for facts; to care about the vulnerable and object to their exploitation; to embrace the Other and welcome the stranger; to favor nonviolent solutions over aggression. Most of all, those whose awareness is rooted in Spirit see that we're part of something bigger than ourselves. Not by way of dogma or belief—although beliefs matter—but through direct perception of the unity that pervades the limitless diversity of life. This is vital because that sense of deep, unbreakable connection is an antidote to the tribalism and petty loyalties that threaten to destroy us. Without inflating our expectations, it seems reasonable to assume that, in these tenuous times, the world will only benefit if spiritual awareness finds expression in real-life decisions and actions.

My primary goal for this book was to offer practical ways to stay safe, stable, and spiritually sane in a world gone crazy. If I succeeded even a little, you will also have a sturdier platform from which to help reduce the insanity. What form that action takes is up to you. Don't be paralyzed by the enormity of the problems we face; do something, anything, to express your spiritual values in a context even slightly larger than the one you normally operate in. Every gesture made with love and decency matters. "Do not overlook tiny good actions, thinking they are of no benefit," the Buddha advised. "Even tiny drops of water in the end will fill a huge vessel."

Your drop is needed. It might make a bigger splash than you think.

Acknowledgments

I want to thank Patty Gift and her colleagues at Hay House for recognizing the possibilities of the book and getting behind it in a timely manner. I'm particularly grateful to my editor, Anne Barthel, who helped me conceptualize the book in its formative phase and astutely spotted manuscript weaknesses along the way. Deep thanks also to my longtime agent and friend, Lynn Franklin, whose unwavering support over the years has been a blessing. I'm grateful also to the friends who helped me think the book through and offered their own insights.

Special thanks to the dear friends and family members whose emotional support was invaluable. Most of all, I'm grateful to my wife, Lori Deutsch, for her encouragement and sharp editorial feedback, not to mention the indispensable health-care expertise that helped me maintain strength and clarity under deadline pressure. Writing is a solitary profession, but raising a book takes a small village of wise and caring souls—who also, by the way, help keep us sane in crazy times.

About the Author

Philip Goldberg has been studying the world's spiritual traditions for more than 50 years, as a practitioner, teacher, and writer. He is the author or co-author of more than 20 books, published in more than a dozen languages, including *The Intuitive Edge*; *Get Out of Your Own Way*; and *Roadsigns on the Spiritual Path: Living at the Heart of Paradox*. His 2010 book *American Veda: From Emerson and the Beatles to Yoga and Meditation, How Indian Spirituality Changed the West* chronicles the remarkable influence of India's traditional spiritual teachings on the West and was named one of the top 10 religion books of the year by both *Huffington Post* and the American Library Association's *Booklist*. His most recent book, published by Hay House, was *The Life of Yogananda: The Story of the Yogi Who Became the First Modern Guru*. A screenwriter and published novelist (*This Is Next Year*), Phil is a member of the Writers Guild of America and the Authors Guild.

An ordained interfaith minister, spiritual counselor, and meditation teacher trained in 1970 by

Maharishi Mahesh Yogi, Phil is an illuminating and entertaining public speaker who has presented at yoga centers and festivals, universities, retreat centers, religious and spiritual institutions, and other venues throughout the United States and India. He leads workshops on Indian sacred texts, meditation, and related topics, both in person and online. He blogs, mainly about religion and spirituality, in *Elephant Journal* and contributes regularly to *Spirituality & Health* online about the intersection of spirituality and social issues.

Phil has been interviewed by a variety of newspapers, magazines, and radio and television outlets, and appears onscreen in the award-winning documentary *Awake: The Life of Yogananda*. He also conducts journeys to sacred India through his company, American Veda Tours, and co-hosts the popular *Spirit Matters* podcast, which features interviews with a diverse array of spiritual teachers and leaders. Born and raised in Brooklyn, he now lives in Los Angeles with his wife, acupuncturist Lori Deutsch. His website is www.PhilipGoldberg.com.

Hay House Titles of Related Interest

YOU CAN HEAL YOUR LIFE, the movie,
starring Louise Hay & Friends
(available as a 1-DVD program, an expanded 2-DVD set,
and an online streaming video)
Learn more at www.hayhouse.com/louise-movie

THE SHIFT, the movie,
starring Dr. Wayne W. Dyer
(available as a 1-DVD program, an expanded 2-DVD set,
and an online streaming video)
Learn more at www.hayhouse.com/the-shift-movie

■■■

*LET YOUR FEARS MAKE YOU FIERCE: How to Turn
Common Obstacles into Seeds for Growth,* by Koya Webb

*MORE BEAUTIFUL THAN BEFORE: How
Suffering Transforms Us,* by Steve Leder

*RESILIENCE FROM THE HEART: The Power to
Thrive in Life's Extremes,* by Gregg Braden

*THE UNIVERSE ALWAYS HAS A PLAN: The 10
Golden Rules of Letting Go,* by Matt Kahn

All of the above are available at your local bookstore,
or may be ordered by contacting Hay House (see next page).

■■■

We hope you enjoyed this Hay House book. If you'd like to receive our online catalog featuring additional information on Hay House books and products, or if you'd like to find out more about the Hay Foundation, please contact:

HAY HOUSE

Hay House, Inc., P.O. Box 5100, Carlsbad, CA 92018-5100
(760) 431-7695 or (800) 654-5126
(760) 431-6948 (fax) or (800) 650-5115 (fax)
www.hayhouse.com® • www.hayfoundation.org

■ ■ ■

Published in Australia by: Hay House Australia Pty. Ltd.,
18/36 Ralph St., Alexandria NSW 2015
Phone: 612-9669-4299 • *Fax:* 612-9669-4144
www.hayhouse.com.au

Published in the United Kingdom by: Hay House UK, Ltd.,
The Sixth Floor, Watson House, 54 Baker Street, London W1U 7BU
Phone: +44 (0)20 3927 7290 • *Fax:* +44 (0)20 3927 7291
www.hayhouse.co.uk

Published in India by: Hay House Publishers India,
Muskaan Complex, Plot No. 3, B-2, Vasant Kunj, New Delhi 110 070
Phone: 91-11-4176-1620 • *Fax:* 91-11-4176-1630
www.hayhouse.co.in

■ ■ ■

Access New Knowledge.
Anytime. Anywhere.

Learn and evolve at your own pace
with the world's leading experts.

www.hayhouseU.com